THE OLD DAD

Vincent Capodicci, Jr.

DORRANCE
PUBLISHING CO
EST. 1920
PITTSBURGH, PENNSYLVANIA 15238

Dorrance Publishing Co
585 Alpha Drive
Pittsburgh, PA 15238
Visit our website at *www.dorrancebookstore.com*

ISBN: 978-1-6491-3145-4
EISBN: 978-1-6491-3667-1

Table of Contents

Introduction

....

BEFORE WE START, I need to get this off my chest. Never in my life did I think I'd be sitting down writing a book. Hell, when I was a kid, it took my stepmom Bev's multiple threats to my life to get me to read a book, and that's not taking into account summer reading requirements while in elementary school.

Then one day it all changed. During the summer of 1985 between the 7th and 8th grade, Bev decided to give it one last shot before throwing in the towel and letting me go down the path of stupidity. She picked up a book on the D-Day invasion of Normandy and BAM! that was all it took.

If I remember correctly, the book was about 400 pages long. I don't remember the title of it, but I do remember it had some pictures, which was a big plus. When I first picked it up, I had no idea it would change my life, leading me down the road of military history books while also opening my mind to reading in general.

I finished the book in about four days, and after proudly telling Bev what I'd done, I remember her responding that I was full of shit (or something like that) and that she would read the book as well and quiz me on it. Being true to her word, she did as she promised, and during a thirty-minute inquisition on the who, what, when, why, and where of it, she realized that, (1) I had read the book, and (2) she may be onto something here with me.

The remainder of the summer I read three more books on military history. Since that time I have "literally" read thousands of books and not just on military history. The older I got, the more curious I became, and books related to adventure became the object of my passion.

This "new me," as I like to call it, represented a major transformation. It not only led me to becoming an honor student but even to this day, some thirty years later, I can't stop reading. And while a Nook has replaced many paperbacks, my library continues to grow, from such classics as *Tom Sayer* to my ultimate favorite book, *20000 Leagues Under the Sea.*

And now as I write my own book, I hope to pass my love of reading on to my son so that reading becomes a gateway for him to find his true life passions. I know that reading did that for me, leading me to serve in the US Navy and opening me up to many other adventures that continue to this very day.

Collin, this is for you!

CHAPTER I

The Big News

....

AS I GET OLDER, it seems harder and harder to remember things. Just ask my wife! On Memorial Day, September 3, 2012, a suicide bomber drove a vehicle filled with 500 pounds of explosives into my armored Toyota Land Cruiser. I was in Peshawar, Pakistan, as a Security Protection Specialist with the Department of State Bureau of Diplomatic Security.

It may not have been my time to die, but the incident forever changed my life. It left me with a brachial artery tear in my left arm, broken ribs on the left side of my body, ruptured ear drums, glass- and gravel-embedded cuts, and a traumatic brain injury (TBI). The bones and cuts healed, but I now need a hearing aid in my right ear and the TBI? Let's just say I forget a lot of stuff, and if it wasn't for my ever-present notebook and the memo app on my iPhone, God only knows how much more would disappear. I did maintain my long-term memory, but short-term loss is the issue, which I'm sure drives my wife and coworkers a little crazy at times.

What I find funny about all this is how I am no longer able to type. In the past I could type 200 – 250 words a minute. Not too shabby! But now I just peck at the keyboard. And if it wasn't for spell-check, there's no telling what type of gibberish would end up on the page.

One thing I do remember: the day my wife told me she was pregnant, like it happened thirty seconds ago. May 13, 2018, started out like a typical Mother's Day. Since it was the first time in a few years that I was home from Afghanistan to celebrate it with my mom, Jerri, we decided to also invite my mother-in-law Cindy over for the weekend. Both my mom and mother-in-law get along great, so it's always nice to bring the two of them together.

It was raining that day, and I was outside working on a broken pipe to the pool house. My two dogs, Winnie and Clarice, decided to keep me company, or maybe they just liked rolling in the mud. I was almost finished when my wife came out to get me; it was time to open up gifts. I dutifully said, "Okay," stopped what I was doing, and followed her into the house. But something wasn't right; when we got inside, she had her video camera out, and all I thought was "Oh crap, what did she buy them and how much did it cost?"

Jerri and Cindy started opening gifts and at least to my eye none of them were video-camera worthy: some Avon products, Yankee Candles, you know, nothing too crazy or extreme.

We were almost done, my wife still filming, when she handed me a small, brown, cardboard box from the beauty products company Sephora. I had no clue what was inside it but thanked her and said I would open it later. She sweetly asked me to open the box now and kept filming.

Only a few pieces of tape were holding it closed, so I easily popped it open. When I looked inside, it took me a few seconds to realize what was there. But when I did, trying to describe the look on my face would not do it justice; you would have to watch the video where you would see Vincent turn pale and go blank. I remember asking my wife if this was a joke. "Not on your life," she firmly replied.

As what I saw started to officially register, I experienced pure joy and terror all at once, but my huge, trademark, shit-eating grin could not be suppressed. As this was happening, my mom and Cindy were asking "What…!?" and then I pulled from the box two positive pregnancy tests and a three-pack of baby onesies.

For my mom, this was her first grandchild; for Cindy, this would be her fourth, but the joy in both of their eyes touches me to this very day. Heck, I'd be lying if I said I still didn't get a little teary-eyed. My wife Kelly, on the other hand, was probably feeling mixed emotions. You see, she and I had a plan, and children weren't an immediate part of it. Since we got married in 2013, we always agreed that we wouldn't try for a child, but we also wouldn't prevent it. And so when Kelly decided to go back to school to study mortuary science, we started to take more preventive measures to avoid her getting pregnant. Kelly continued her studies while and I took my current position with the State Department working in the US Embassy Kabul Tactical Operations Center (TOC). In August 2016 Kelly and I closed on a historical farmhouse dating back to the 1700s in Hampton, CT.

The plan was going great until I returned home from Afghanistan for a visit in mid-April 2018 fully pumped to see my girl and, well, we just let it all flow. A doctor's appointment later confirmed the date of conception as

April 17, 2018—the very day I got back. We would officially be parents on or around Jan 17, 2019.

And so our joy was tinged with some anxiety. Kelly's pregnancy pretty much threw a wrench in all of our plans, especially for Kelly finishing up school. I was honestly scared shitless. Being responsible for a wife, a stepson, a couple of dogs, and a cat had already filled my plate especially with the amount of time I was away from home due to my job. As happy as I was, I felt bad knowing that Kelly would take on the biggest burden of running the household when I gone.

From that point on, everything was pretty much a blur, but the pregnancy itself was going smoothly with a few perfunctory doctors' appointments and some basic family planning. No one knew other than our mothers, and Kelly and I decided we would tell immediate family only and avoid any announcements on social media.

I broke my notification process down into two groups: those to call and those I could get away with sending an email. I come from a typically large East Coast Italian family, so it was emotional chaos when the news broke—to say there were lots of tears and joy would be an understatement. This was especially true for my Aunt Jo. As the oldest of three boys, I was de facto head of the family after my father passed away in 2000, but my brothers and cousins never really paid much attention to that. And once my grandmother passed away in 2012, we put aside the traditional way of doing things and just rolled with what was. But Aunt Jo still sticks to the traditional family way of doing things, taking over as head Capodicci after my grandmother's passing. And so with her oldest nephew soon to be a dad, she responded with a full Italian meltdown, both very happy for me and very proud.

Some Family History

My brothers, my cousins, and I were not the marrying type. I didn't get hitched until I was forty, and my second eldest brother, Chris, waited until his thirties. As for my youngest brother, Sal, and my cousins Brian and Tara, they remain happily single. My brother Chris was the first to have kids, and his wife Dorrie was pregnant with their second when Kelly joined the party.

There is a seven-year age difference between each of my brothers. I remember growing up hearing my dad say he planned it this way so he would always have someone to mow his lawn. He instilled in us boys the importance of family and that, as brothers, we should always look out for each other. The three of us have never had a big disagreement and are very close. My brother

Chris and I live about thirty-five minutes away from each other and, up until about a year ago, Sal lived close as well until he moved to Tampa, Florida.

Besides her mom, Cindy, the rest of Kelly's family did not seem too enthusiastic about the pregnancy which surprised me. Kelly has two brothers, Sean and Christopher. Sean is the oldest and happily married with two kids. Christopher is more like my brother Sal. With the exception of living at home, he still loves the single life and at the end of the day enjoys fishing and a good beer. I get along with both of them, but due to Christopher being single, I spend more time with him at the shooting range or tipping a few local beers whenever we get the chance.

I think the person who surprised me the most was my father-in-law, Geno. I absolutely love Geno to death; he is one of the hardest working old-school type of man I have ever met. To this day, I still don't know why he wasn't happy when Kelly told him about the news. Fortunately that all changed once our son was born, but his initial conflict remains a mystery.

In the beginning I thought it might be something about me. I am far from a perfect husband, but I'm pretty good (though you'll have to ask Kelly) and have always shown my wife respect and love that come from the bottom of my heart. I've been blessed with a successful career and am able to provide for my family above and beyond their needs. I'm a little rough around the edges, but hey, I spent more than fifteen years in the Navy and the last fourteen years overseas, so I never back down from a fight, and I guess I use the word "f—k" a lot. But does this make me a bad person?

After notifying immediate family and friends, life, for the most part, went back to normal. With the exception of some prenatal vitamins, Kelly's lifestyle didn't really change, and we always had healthy eating habits. I was getting ready to head back to Afghanistan for a ninety-day rotation, so we already had an idea of when I would be home again. One of the perks of my job is that I can schedule leave about a year in advance, so I knew I'd be home again in August, back for Thanksgiving, and then right after Christmas about a week before Kelly's due date. If the baby decided to come early, we'd have some wiggle room for that.

When taking leave while employed by the State Department, there is always a lot more flexibility compared to someone serving overseas in the military. If, for example, there's a family emergency back home, there is usually no need for a Red Cross message; we can go directly to our supervisor and HR and pretty much be on a plane in a couple of hours. This is mainly because, in Afghanistan, we use civilian airlines and don't have to rely on the more typical

Space "A" military flights. The connection flights are a little tricky, but even worst-case scenario you can get from Kabul to your home in about twenty-seven hours.

As Kelly and I discussed next steps, we started to compile lists of what we need to do to get ready for the baby. One thing we agreed on was that we did not want to know the sex of the baby until he or she came out so it would be a total surprise. To tell you the truth, we kind of figured it would be a girl because Kelly already had a son and, for some weird reason, most of the guys in my line of work have girls.

So with all the initial prep and planning underway, it was time to pack my bag and head back to Afghanistan. Kelly had already made her first OBGYN appointment, and of course it was the day I left, but that's usually how it goes.

CHAPTER 2

In the Beginning

·····························

I WAS FORTY-FOUR when I found out my wife was having a baby, and to say I was a little freaked out is an understatement. Most of my friends already had families and were in there mid- to late-twenties when they started, so now I am thinking, *What the hell am I going to do?* My father had Sal, my youngest brother, when he was forty and passed away when he was fifty-two. My dad was a typically heavy-set Italian guy, and many of the men on the Capodicci side of the family die in their fifties. My brothers and I always joked about this, but now here I was, well into my forties, and having a kid.

On a more positive note, I did a lot of research and discovered that in this day and age, it's quite common for men to have children in their forties, so I started to feel a little better. I was more worried about my wife, though she's ten years younger than me and very healthy and the risk is a lot less. In fact, neither one of us would score high on a risk assessment. I'm 5 6 and weight about 140 pounds; Kelly is 5 even and her weight, well, I will say she's petite because writing down her weight here would surely get me killed. We are both physically fit, eat healthy, don't smoke, and are considered social drinkers. But we both still talked about that worst-case scenarios.

And so, even though it all looked good, I still have fears and have no idea how I made it this far in life. I've not lived a normal life; in fact I've lived a unique life. My childhood was typical in a kinda-sorta way. My parents divorced when I was seven, and my dad remarried. My stepmother Bev and I did not get along, and I'm not out of line to imagine there were probably many nights when she stood over my sleeping body contemplating my fate with a pillow in her hands. When all was said and done, though, she had a huge impact on how I grew up. I learned about the importance of a solid work ethic, taking responsibility for one's actions, and believing in yourself. I would not be where I am today if it wasn't for her. I always tell people I have two mothers and because of that, I am very fortunate.

My father had two children with Bev, Chris and Sal. The way my father brought us up, there were no such things as step- or half brothers; we were just brothers. It was because of this that my brothers and I are still close to this day, though that didn't mean we didn't do typical brother things while growing up, even though we were each seven years apart. Chris, for example, ended up with his ass hanging out of a window once; and Sal, well, there was an incident with a duffel bag and some stairs. But I'll save those stories for another time.

My birth mother, Jerri, never remarried and used her divorce to catch up on lost youth since she and my father got married at a young age. In the end, my mother was always there for me and ensured I always had everything I could possibly need. This turned out to be the perfect parenting balance: my mom gave me the freedom to do what I wanted, and Bev gave me structure, which I guess makes me a pretty well-balanced person.

As for my dad, he took me everywhere and did the same with my brothers. He was a pure badass—electrical engineer by day, burly biker on the weekends—and one of the greatest men I have ever known. I've always felt bad for my youngest brother, Sal, because he was only twelve when our father passed away and didn't get to experience a lot of the things Chris and I did. To this very day I sometimes get mad at my dad for missing out on so much of our lives after he passed away, but nineteen years later, I miss him more than anything.

Growing up we had a cabin in upstate New York where we spent the summer and most holidays. My father encouraged us to be adventurous and always supported the things we did. He was an avid hunter, which I never really enjoyed; I found walking in the woods more exciting than sitting in a tree stand waiting to shoot animals. But that experience led me to becoming a Boy Scout. Unlike most kids my age, scouting was a huge part of my life. Not a single summer went by when I didn't spend time away from home at camp or on some high-adventure trip. Ultimately, the support I received from my family helped guide me to achieving the rank of Eagle Scout. It was also due to this support that I added skydiving, scuba diving, and rock climbing to my adventures as I turned sixteen.

My parents never really pushed college on me as an option, but I wanted to join the military after high school so I could jump out of airplanes and blow shit up. I did try college for awhile, but it wasn't for me—at least not yet. I had no idea that later in life I'd end up with two bachelor's and a master's degree. Go figure.

Joining the military and serving in the US Navy turned out to be my true calling and a decision that helped me get to where I am today. Well, that and the "War on Terror." I was a hospital corpsman for over fifteen years from August 1994 to September 2009 on both active duty with the Naval Special Warfare Command in Coronado, California, and the reserves serving in the 24th Marine Division in Kansas City, Missouri. I would have been happy to stay where I was, but the travel and inconsistent days off started to burn me out.

During this period, the Global War on Terror (GWOT) was heating up, and Iraq was becoming the new area of concern. One day a friend of mine, Jerri, approached me at the Naval Amphibious Base (NAB) swimming pool in San Diego and asked me what I have been up to. I got him up to speed, and then he asked me if I'd ever considered working for Blackwater.

"No really," I replied. One of the main reasons is that they mostly recruited Tier 1 operators—members of Special Operations, the guys who kicked in doors and pulled triggers—and I didn't fit that category. However, since I was an experienced hospital corpsman with a solid reputation in the Naval Special Warfare (NSWC) community, he said I would be a good candidate. That night after a few beers with Jerri and a detailed rundown on what I would be doing, where I'd be working, and, more importantly, how much money I'd be making, I had a training class date and an opening to the world of Private Military Contracting (PMC).

At the time I was in a serious relationship with my girlfriend, Krista. I hadn't even unpacked my bags when I told her the news, which meant I would be gone as much as if I was on active duty, and to say she wasn't pleased is an understatement. In fact, she was really angry and that very same night gave me an ultimatum: her or Blackwater. I was very focused on my career and have always been a very patriotic person, so as long as we were fighting two wars, there was no way I was going to miss out. It took me about two seconds to tell her I'd be out of the house in two weeks. The decision broke my heart, but I knew that working as a PMC with Blackwater was my calling no matter how dangerous the job.

The next two weeks were a blur, but I was on sixty days of terminal leave from the Navy, which gave me time to find a new apartment and get ready to start my training with Blackwater. It was December of 2004. Fortunately, Krista and I managed to remain friends and to this day there are no hard feelings between us. She's a good person, and we never regretted the time we were together. Now, when she reads this book she may get pissed because when we were together we adopted a dog, Curry, and I think I missed the dog more than Krista!

Training with Blackwater was a blast, and during their academy we were put through the wringer. Many of our instructors were straight out of SWAT and Special Forces units and to say we trained hard would not give them justice. During the eight-week training course, we probably blew through 50,000 rounds of ammo shooting just about any type of weapon you could think off. Every morning when I woke up, my trigger finger was a swollen blister that needed to be popped if I wanted to fit it in the trigger well of my weapons.

In April 2005, three weeks after I completed training, I was on my first contract in Baghdad. Fourteen years later I'm still here!

Working with Blackwater was amazing, and as dangerous as it was, I worked with some of the best guys I've ever come across. There aren't many professionals that you can trust with your life, but my military experience with Blackwater was one of those times. Also, my role as a contractor opened up a lot of new opportunities. Working in Iraq, I was able to conduct "High-Profile" and "Low-Profile" protective security operations. Crossing over from the protection side into "Counter Assault" gave me a different perspective. The most rewarding contract I worked on was as an aerial door gunner providing coverage to our teams on the ground. I can honestly say that if being a door gunner was still an option, I would still be hanging my ass out the side of a helicopter with a belt-fed machine gun in my hands.

As rewarding as it was working for Blackwater, the contracting world was changing and it was time to move on to bigger and better things. My next big accomplishment was getting hired on directly as an officer with the Departments of State (DOS) Bureau of Diplomatic Security (DS) as a Security Protective Specialist (SPS). As a direct hire, I was now responsible for the general oversight of PMCs working for the DOS. This position came into play after the infamous 2007 Nisar Square incident in Baghdad, where PMCs were accused of firing on innocent Iraqi civilians. This is not the time nor place to talk about the different opinions of what actually went down, but unless you were actually there, I encourage you to do your research before coming to any conclusions.

I enjoyed my time as an SPS, which ultimately placed me at the US Embassy in Kabul, not far from Peshawar where my life would be forever changed. Whenever I look at the photos of the vehicle I was in when the car bomb hit us, there is no possible explanation of how I survived. This one instant made me believe that God has a plan for us, and sometimes it's just not your time to go.

I ended up in the Tactical Operations Center (TOC), which I never thought would happen but sooner or later you have to move aside and let the next generation step in. So I hung up my gun belt and got off the road. This made my wife Kelly very happy. Being assigned to the TOC at an embassy as big as Kabul is kind of like waking up every day with a straight kick to the nuts. With over 7,000 direct hires and contract personnel working in an active war zone, let's just say every day is different and sometimes you literally sit back scratching your head over the crazy-ass things that people do. What, I often wondered, is wrong with them?!

Nevertheless, I believe that the decisions one makes, along with the decision made for you, both good and bad, ultimately take you in the right direction sooner or later. For example, until I met Kelly, I had no desire to get married or start a family. Hell, when I was working as a PMC with Blackwater and even as an SPS, I never hesitated to volunteer for a mission and always believed it was better to go out in a blaze of gunfire then fat and lazy in a recliner. Who would have known that everything would change the day I meet Kelly?

Kelly and I met through internet dating. When we first started talking, I was wrapping up my sixth and final year with Blackwater in Afghanistan right before I started SPS training in January 2011. After emailing back and forth for about a month, I think she was ready to give up due to me being in Afghanistan and then some whirlwind travel from Kabul to home to DC to start my SPS class on March 13, 2011. If I remember correctly, Kelly decided to give her ex-boyfriend another try and broke off any further communication between us.

About a month or so later, I received an email from Kelly wanting to talk, which caught me off guard. I let her know I'd be home in June when I finished training and would have a couple of weeks off before heading back to Iraq. We continued to chat and set up our first date to meet. We decided she would meet me at my condo and then we would go out for dinner later.

To say I was a little nervous would be a lie; it was much worse. Due to the nature of my work, I rarely got an opportunity to date except when I was home and you never know who you were going to meet. When Kelly showed up, she called me so I could buzz her in at the gate. Since my condo was off the road a bit, I wanted to meet her on the road or she might have driven right by. All I remember is this full-size Toyota Tundra pulling up and this tiny little blonde girl stepping out and thinking, "Wow, she's cute!"

I'm pretty shy so I just invited her into the condo and showed her around. I didn't want her to feel uncomfortable, so rather than hanging out in the condo I asked if she would like to go swimming. I enjoyed being at the pool and just talking, and after a couple of hours we went out to dinner. Since it was July, I wanted to take her to a place where we could eat outside, so we went to this restaurant in Farmington, Connecticut, called Apricots. Since she lived about two hours away in Brookfield, Massachusetts, she decided to head home after dinner, and we planned another date before I left for Iraq the following week.

Our second date was a blast and definitely not average. We went skydiving, something I hadn't done in about eight months. We met up at Jump Town USA in Orange, Massachusetts, where Kelly made her first—and last—jump. For me it was jump #3,216—I'd been jumping out of planes since I was sixteen, and it was no big deal. I used my GoPro to film the jump, and afterwards we decided to go out for lunch and play some miniature golf. Since Kelly had to work that night, she went home early, and since I was headed back to Iraq, we decided to keep talking and make plans for when I came back in October.

We continued to date and on September 6, 2013, were married by a justice of the peace and decided not to tell anyone. Originally we had planned to get married in front of our friends and family the following summer, but since I was stationed in Peshawar at the time, Kelly wanted to go back to school to become a mortician, and it just made sense that she move to Connecticut with her son Brett and become a full-time student while I was away in Pakistan. This way I would also be able to claim both her and Brett as dependents when she quit her job and went back to school. We still planned to have a big wedding for our families.

After that we fell into a routine of balancing marriage. working overseas, being a student, and helping Brett adjust to moving and starting a new school. The rest, as they say, is history, and here we are, over six years later, and a lot has sure changed.

CHAPTER 3
The Midwife Dilemma
··

LEAVING HOME for Kabul in May 2018 was quite different this time than in the past. Kelly and I had made Hampton, Connecticut, our new home, and living in a historic farmhouse with thirty acres of land started changing my perspective. I began to really enjoy being home, and with Kelly now pregnant, my mind started racing with new scenarios. She was only in her first month of the pregnancy, though, so we had plenty of time to figure things out.

During my first couple of weeks back in Kabul, Kelly and I began brainstorming a game plan on what needed to be done both before and after the baby arrived. I also needed to line up my leaves so I would be home for Thanksgiving and able to take family leave when the baby was due. We also needed to come up with a name, which turned out to be more difficult than I anticipated. I wanted to name the baby Dominic if it was a boy, and Kelly wanted no part of that. So we decided to put the name thing to the side and wing it when the time came.

Doctor's appointments became the new norm for Kelly, which she juggled along with school and Brett, who was about to turn thirteen, so she had her hands full. Since her doctor had placed her in a high-risk category because she was over thirty-five and had high blood pressure during her pregnancy with Brett, she had more than the usual number of appointments. For the most part, though, the pregnancy was going according to plan, and Kelly's body was adjusting to having a bun in the oven. Her mental and emotional state, however, was another matter entirely.

As most women probably know, as goes a pregnancy, so goes the moods of the mother-to-be. Kelly is pretty levelheaded, but she's also stubborn as hell. Throw in a new storm of hormones, and I swear to God, whenever I called home from Afghanistan, I had no clue who would be answering the phone. Would it Kelly the love of my life or this demon who now possessed her? I felt bad for Brett because he was in the impact zone and got the brunt of the mood swings while I was more than 7,000 miles away in another part of the world. I can joke about this now, but it was safer for me in war-torn Afghanistan than it was back home in Connecticut.

As I was saying, Kelly's pregnancy was pretty normal: morning sickness, constant exhaustion, swollen feet, the usual stuff. Because she was "high risk," it was recommended that she get an ultrasound and anatomy scan every two weeks. We both agreed that it was better to be safe than sorry. Overall, her appointments were going well and everything was looking good. The only thing left to be done was deciding how and where the birth would take place. Would it be in a traditional hospital or at home using a midwife?

I preferred the traditional route. After spending fifteen years as a Navy Corpsman and six years as a medic with Blackwater, I was well aware of the advancements in medical care, especially when it came to trauma. I can see the argument that giving birth is a non-trauma type event, but with Kelly being high risk, my rational mind thought, "Why take the chance?" Another reason I wanted a hospital birth was based on my own experience delivering a couple of babies—once in the Navy and once when I was with Blackwater. Childbirth may be beautiful, but it's also freakin' messy!

My first experience delivering a child was in 1995 while a junior corpsman assigned to the emergency room at Great Lakes Naval Hospital. I was assisting the ER doctor and nurse during a night shift rotation when a young woman was brought in ready to pop. Since GLNH was a training hospital, both the nurse and the doctor let me do most of the delivery, and while there were fluids of all kinds and the little tyke was awfully slippery, everything went smoothly enough. That experience was truly some of the best training one could ask for.

The second delivery was a different story. It took place while I was protecting personnel at the International Republic Institute (IRI), which is responsible for helping the Iraqis run their very first election. Working in Baghdad during that first election was a unique experience. The IRI contract had us living in the city in a neighborhood area we called "the penis" because if you sketched it on a map, that's what it looked like. During the elections, security increased as did travel restrictions and a curfew that went from 2000 military time (8 p.m.) to 0600 hours (6 a.m.) pretty much seven days a week. To be caught on the roads during the curfew was not only dangerous for American security contractors but more so for Iraqi citizens. Most of the locals appreciated the extra security we brought there.

It was sometime in October 2006. In addition to my security work, I was the senior medic and ran our medical clinic. It wasn't much more than a small room with a bed, but we had access to whatever medicine and equipment we needed to treat anything from the common cold to a gunshot wound. All the medics working IRI with me we're former military medical with either infantry or special operations backgrounds. The locals would come to our house quite often for help, especially during the curfew hours.

On one particular evening, a local guard came into my room and told me that one of the neighbors needed help and to come right away. After jumping out of bed and throwing on some flip-flops, I made the short jog to our clinic. I had no idea what I was getting into, but when I walked into the clinic, there on the bed lay a pregnant woman with her husband soaking wet from her water breaking. I remember saying to myself, "Holy shit."

With Iraq being a Muslim country, I couldn't just jump right in and put my hands on her body. So I had our translator ask the husband in Arabic if I could help his wife. This was a young couple in their midtwenties. The husband said yes, that as long as I saved his wife and child, I could do whatever I needed, and he would ask for Allah to forgive later. So in typical doc fashion, I assessed the situation and quickly realized that she was crowning—the baby was on its way out, and there was nothing to do except get ready for it.

It had been almost ten years since I'd delivered a baby, and I was red-alert nervous, because, other than a refresher course every two years for my medic recertification, I'd delivered no real babies and now here I was, running the whole show! Fortunately it turned out to be a textbook delivery. All I had to do was suction the baby's airway, give the mother some oxygen, wrap the baby up in a blanket, and monitor the vitals until the parents could drive to the hospital after the curfew lifted at 0600. But even an "easy" delivery is tense and messy, with more blood and shit and mucus and fluids than I would have ever thought possible.

Don't get me wrong. I am very grateful to have been able to take part in this birth. But now that my wife was considering a home birth, the last thing I wanted to deal with in my own home was *all of that*. The possibility of having to take my wife to the hospital if there was any type of emergency just amped up my fear because anyone from the Northeast knows that the weather in January can be brutal.

One of the things I love about my wife is that she doesn't take any shit from me, which helps keep me in line. She supports my job and my various adventures but still holds me accountable for being a responsible adult. The downside is that she can be a little hardheaded, and when she makes up her mind, that's pretty much it. But in our good old-fashioned grown-up way of doing things, we always tend to reach a neutral understanding and end up getting at least some of what we want. You give a little to get a little.

Now back to the whole midwife conversation. Under no circumstances would some voodoo priestess come into my home and deliver my child in a living room in the middle of winter with two dogs, a cat, and a thirteen-year-old under my roof. Still, I wanted to give Kelly the benefit of the doubt. She did the research, met with several midwives in the area, and made a final choice for me to meet when I came home again in August. We also agreed that if we went with the midwife, Kelly would still see her OBGYN doctor all the way until the end of the pregnancy and if anything weird happened during the birth, we'd head to the hospital.

When I came home in August, the three of us met. I won't use the midwife's real name because in the second part of the story—which I will share later in the book—she turned out to be crazy. And so she doesn't sue me, I will call her Janet.

Our first meeting with Janet was surprisingly pleasant. I had my questions ready, and truth be told, I was looking for any excuse to pull the plug. But she seemed very professional in a hippie sort of way. My initial questions concerned the usual medical certifications and experience delivering babies. We discussed possible complications and what would be done in case of an emergency. She not only answered all my questions but agreed with me to have Kelly keep seeing her regular doctor throughout the pregnancy. It was all enough to put me at ease.

The first red flag I missed was her billing. The average cost of a home birth in Connecticut is roughly $7,000, but Janet had a cash policy of $4,400 if paid directly to her and not through an insurance company. She would still bill the insurance company $7000, which for my provider would come off the deductible. I figured that for what I pay out of pocket for health insurance annually, any break I could get would be a good thing, especially with how Obamacare had screwed me. Now that I look back at it, by paying her cash, she likely hid a bit of the money for tax purposes, but I'm not the IRS, so what do I care.

Janet didn't have an official contract; it was more of a written agreement that was vague about what services she offered and her major responsibilities. Kelly and I offered to pay her $1,000 initially and then a portion of the remaining amount every other week when Kelly had a visit with her until the balance was paid in full. Janet agreed, and we decided to move forward.

In the beginning everything was fine. Kelly went to her OBGYN appointments followed by a session with Janet. The pregnancy was going well and there were no issues with the baby. Although Kelly wasn't putting on much weight, the fetus was growing normally and both the doctor and Janet agreed there was no reason for alarm. Janet even came to the house and conducted a couple of home visits to get an idea of where Kelly would deliver and what equipment we'd need for the smoothest possible delivery. My main question was who would clean up after the bloody mess. Janet assured me that during the whole process, she and her assistant would take care of everything.

The second red flag we should have seen came up when Kelly went to a meeting organized by Janet, who likes to have monthly get-togethers so that current and past clients can meet each other. Since I was back in Afghanistan, Kelly had to go by herself. During the meeting they did the usual meet-and-greet and people talked about the pros and cons of home birth. Kelly wanted to know why some of them chose home birth over the traditional way. According to Kelly, the answers seemed unsurprising—the warmth and familiarity of being at home with family. One lady's answer shocked Kelly a little. She preferred home birth because she liked to smoke marijuana during pregnancy and when she had her last child at the hospital, the Department of Child Services got involved because she popped hot on her piss test after the birth, and so did the baby.

When Kelly told me this, I was immediately turned off again and wanted no part of these hippies. My biggest concern was why the midwife would take on people like this as clients after learning about the drug-use pregnancy. Janet assured us she was only concerned for the health of the baby and couldn't force parents not to use drugs—though she recommended they stop during the pregnancy. Kelly believed her because, like I said, she was really nice and very pleasant to work with up to this point.

The third and final red flag was the home birth video, which went over the whole experience and why people chose this way of bringing their child into the world. I won't say the video was a bad thing, but you gotta remember: I'd been overseas fighting a war since 2001 and I'd become pretty skeptical about anything that came off as woo-woo. At first the video seemed okay; it went into the setup and how a home birth should go. There were interviews with home birthers about their experiences both good and bad—some that went smoothly and others where emergencies required a fast drive to the hospital. That part actually brought me some comfort, and I was starting to feel better about it all.

Then came the pictures. As a combat medic serving in both Iraq and Afghanistan, the images of blood and mucus didn't faze me one bit. It was the pictures of entire families in the birthing tub that blew my mind. There was no way in hell I was getting into one of those tubs with my wife and our thirteen-year-old son as that baby popped out for a family picture. Still, I consider myself to be an honorable man, and since Kelly wanted to continue with Janet and the docs as agreed, I'd go along with the home birth. I wasn't going to change my opinion about it, but I wanted to support Kelly.

CHAPTER 4

Home Sweet Home

···

MY NINETY-DAY ROTATION in Kabul flew by and before I knew it, I was on my way home. While I was gone, Kelly and Brett kept up their typical routines including regular doctor visits to monitor the baby. Kelly had a couple of ultrasounds done along with an anatomy scan and it was pretty cool to see how the baby was developing. They were able to determine the sex of the baby, but Kelly and I decided that we wanted to be surprised (and we just assumed we would have a girl). All in all, everything was still good to go.

Whenever I return home from a work rotation, it takes a while to get used to being back, as anyone serving and or working overseas can relate to. I want to make up for lost time and sometimes forget that while I'm away, "normal life" goes on. So what ends up happening is that I come out of the gate at 100 mph and mess up the system that Kelly and Brett maintain while I'm gone. I should take it slower, but since I'm overeager to help for the first week or so, I end up being a royal pain in the ass.

I do enjoy my routines when I'm home, which include getting up early to eat and relax with our dogs Clarice and Winnie. And since I get up early, I have time for a good workout either at the gym or going for a nice long run. I've always been an active person, and since I joined the Navy, working out and staying in shape have been a major part of my life. Several years ago, I started running "obstacle course" races and have actively competed in the Warrior Dash, Tough Mudder, and the Spartan Race.

The rest of the day I spend time with Kelly and Brett and, of course, there's never-ending "honey-do" list that I swear gets longer and longer every time I come home. Not that Kelly isn't doing her part. She's an amazing wife since she not only puts up with me working overseas but manages our home, a thirteen-year-old son, and the animals. Throw in her mortician classes and it's safe to say she has a full plate.

When Kelly and I first met, she was a nursing assistant but wanted to go back to school to become a mortician. She started going part-time right after we got engaged, and she moved to my condo in Torrington and has been plugging away ever since. With me out of town up to nine months a year, though, being a full-time student wasn't possible. On the upside, my jobs have paid the bills and then some, which gives Kelly the opportunity to run the house full-time, go to school part-time, and not have to work. This lessens the burden, but being away from home so much is still hard no matter what.

The pregnancy did throw off Kelly's graduation by a year because we decided not to risk exposing her or the baby to toxic embalming fluids. All the research we came across said it should be avoided and that was plenty enough to convince us. Kelly slowed down her classwork, but if all goes well, she should graduate by the end of the summer 2020 semester.

Up to this point, Kelly continued with all of her OBGYN and midwife appointments. There was still an issue with her not gaining much weight, but no one was concerned since Kelly is naturally petite. Still, both her doctor and the midwife recommended checkups every two weeks as things moved forward.

One of my challenges was balancing my time between making sure Kelly was being taken care of but also hanging with Brett—I didn't want him to feel like a second-class citizen. Since there had been so much focus on Kelly and the baby, the three of us decided to go on a short vacation. We had to be careful on choosing a destination since Kelly had to pee about every five minutes, so we took a trip to Niagara Falls. The drive time from our house to the hotel in Canada was a little over six hours, but there would be plenty of opportunity to make multiple stops on the way.

The trip was a blast, but the summer heat and humidity were hard on Kelly and she couldn't do a lot. In the past we would go to Niagara Falls in the fall. This was our first visit during the summer, and so it was also a lot more crowded. During the day, Brett and I roamed the town and in the evening after dinner we'd all go out since by then it had cooled down. And fortunately we were staying on the Canadian side of the falls, which is 100 times better than the US side. There's a ton more family stuff to do, from driving go-karts to the wax museums. Throw in the arcades and you can play games 24/7.

It was good to get away and a well-needed family break, but once we got back, things started picking up. Kelly still had her appointments, Brett was getting ready for school, and Kelly was finalizing her last semester before the baby came. She had wanted to take both Embalming One and Mortuary Affairs but decided to only take one, which made sense given how she was feeling. I never realized how much pregnancy changes the body and this one was kicking Kelly's ass.

While I was home, we also met with Janet a few times, and I actually started to like her. I still didn't agree with the whole home birth idea, but I wanted to be there for Kelly, and she was sticking to her side of the deal—continuing with her checkups—so a home birth it would be. Janet gave us a list of what we needed to have ready for the birth, and with the exception of a birthing tub, it was all standard equipment: towels, sheets, shower curtains, Chux pads, a home delivery kit, and what I considered some "hippy shit": soft music to set the mood and scented candles. I was still more worried about worst-case scenarios and who would clean up the mess when it was all done. More importantly, we live in a house that was built in the 1700s, so filling up a birthing tub was easier said than done: the floors were old and might not hold the weight; we get our water from a well and 100 gallons might drain it or burn out the pump. So there was a lot on my mind.

In fact, my idea was to just throw a few shower curtains on the bed with some sheets, roll everything up after the birth, and BAM! call it a day. When I suggested this to Kelly, let's just say that if looks could kill, I would not have written what you are reading here today.

I never quite grasped the use of a birthing tub so as I looked into it a little more and it turned out that no one could agree and everyone I asked said something different. Supposedly, the tub reduces the labor process by up to thirty minutes and also helps reduce overall pain. There was a higher rate of agreement that water births help reduce perineal tearing. So I guess that was something. I was also able to confirm that home births do have a higher risk of infant deaths than those in hospitals, which re-triggered my doubts.

We still had plenty of time before the estimated birth date, so I put all these issues to the side and concentrated on supporting to my wife and doing something I was actually looking forward to: getting the baby's room organized, which meant furniture. When it comes to decorating, to say I'm basic would be an understatement. After spending the last eighteen years overseas, what else does one need except a bed with a good mattress? And until I met Kelly, I would eat out of the pot that I cooked in. So in thinking about furniture for the baby's room, I figured that since they'll outgrow everything pretty fast, the simpler the better.

After discussing all of this with Kelly, I was like, okay, let's buy some cheap furniture at Walmart and just throw it away as the baby grows up. Right. The next thing I knew, I was reading up on a place called RH Baby and Child and, well, I was impressed, especially by the prices—more expensive than the bedroom set we already had! No problem. Next stop: the RH Baby store in Boston.

I learned that RH meant Restoration Hardware, and believe it or not, I was already aware of their furniture, and it's pretty classy stuff. And Kelly had been looking at furniture for a while, sending me pictures while I was still back in Afghanistan. So Kelly and I made an appointment and drove to Boston. The furniture was impressive and you do get what you pay for. We thought we had a good idea of what we wanted but decided to get a crib and matching dresser that could be converted as the baby grew and also went with the style of our old home. $5,000 later we had a baby room full of furniture. We also went with "gender neutral" since we didn't know if we were having a boy or a girl. I did throw in a bonus purchase of a kick-ass wooly mammoth rocker. And honestly, the entire experience was pretty smooth, and my wife gets all the credit for that.

Back home we moved some furniture out of the nursery room-to-be and waited for the new furniture to be delivered. Kelly was on her "A" game and already stockpiling diapers, baby wipes, clothes, and everything else needed for a newborn. I saw my mission as trying to talk her out of the home birth, and while I was pretty sure I would lose this battle, quitting isn't something I like to do.

I still thought Kelly would be a lot bigger, but none of the checkups were showing any problems and her hormones were balancing out, so as long as she was happy, we were happy. I also figured that Brett might feel a bit left out with all the focus on the pregnancy, so I included him in much of the planning. But since he just turned thirteen, I was more interested in getting him involved in physical activity so I stared dragging him to my Tough Mudder and Spartan races. One thing I always give Kelly credit for is that, no matter how dumb she thinks I am for crushing my body the way I do in these races, she knows I enjoy them and is very supportive.

Of course you can't just throw a thirteen-year-old kid into one of these brutal events and say "Go!" I decided to just bring him along to see how they are, plus it was good for him to see how I'm able to still push myself physically and mentally even though I am in my midforties. It was also a great opportunity for him to see the kind of support I need when on the course, because in November I was taking him to The World's Toughest Mudder in Atlanta.

Other than getting ready for the baby, life went on as always. Both my mom and mother-in-law were very excited and the clothes and doo-dads kept flowing in—we were drowning in them, which Kelly did an excellent job consolidating into one room. She had to keep reminding me to enjoy this while we can because once the baby arrived, life as we knew it would change instantly for both good and, well, to be determined.

As summer ended, Brett started eighth grade and Kelly went back to school for one last semester. The baby kept growing and the changes in her body started amping up. It was also time to start prepping the house for the fall. As much as we all enjoy having a historic home on thirty acres of land, it's a lot of work to stay on top of. I'd be leaving soon and wouldn't be back until November. By then there could very likely be snow on the ground, so it was time to winter up. Fortunately, I still had some time to relax before heading back, and I wanted to take advantage of it because once I returned for Thanksgiving, the World's Toughest Mudder, and the final push before the baby arrived, I'd be going nonstop.

CHAPTER 5

Afghanistan, Again

....

WHENEVER I'M HOME from Afghanistan, I don't care if my break is three weeks or three months; the time goes by way too fast, and it always seems I just run out of time before I do everything that's on my list. Did I take care of everything I was supposed to do around the house? Did I actually get any time to relax? Did I get to see my friends? And most importantly, did I spend enough time with my family? I can usually answer yes to everything except for taking time to relax, because in the end I often find myself just as worn before heading back out as I was when I got home. That being said, I wouldn't trade it for anything because a busy day at home is a hundred times better than a busy day in Afghanistan.

I have a little routine when I head back to work that not only helps me relax but also gets my head back in the game, because as soon as my feet hit the ground in Kabul there is no transition—I just jump right into it. I usually take the early flight out or Bradley Airport in Windsor Locks, Connecticut, which gets me into Dulles no later than 7:30. Once I check into my Dulles-to-Dubai flight, I grab some breakfast and a few Double IPAs for the thirteen-hour trip. If all goes well on the flight, I start my adjustment back to local time in Kabul, which runs eight to nine hours ahead of Connecticut, depending on the time of year. The beers help me sleep on the plane so when I land in Dubai I can stay awake.

Once I arrive in Dubai, I schedule a twenty-four-hour layover so I can go to a hotel and get as much sun as possible which helps me stay awake and get over any jet lag. Plus, I enjoy Dubai, and it gives me one final chance to feel like a normal person before heading to the US Embassy compound I live on while in Kabul. At the hotel, I hit the steam room for a long, hot shower followed by an afternoon at the rooftop bar getting some sunlight. One of the best things about Dubai is the food; it has any type of food you want. On the same block you can grab sushi or a steak at an Outback, fast food from McDonalds or KFC, or a cup of joe at Starbucks or Tim Hortons. I prefer the local food and have found several hidden restaurants where the locals go.

After a good dinner, I enjoy going back to the rooftop bar of the hotel for a nice glass of wine. Compared to some of our contractors working at the embassy, I'm allowed to drink if I want. But since I'm not much of a drinker, I never have more than a glass of wine or a couple of beers during my work rotation. Even when I'm home, I'm not much of a drinker; I think after my escapades in college and the military, I put my drinking days behind me.

After a good night's sleep and a healthy breakfast, I usually head to the airport for my final flight to Kabul. For those who aren't used to it, Kabul can be an overwhelming experience. But over the years, I've probably made the trip several dozen times, so for me it's become a normal routine. Once I land and clear Customs, I meet with our "expediters" (the re-entry team) for a ride to our airbase and take a helicopter from the base to the helicopter landing zone just a short walk to my room. And just like that, I am back in Kabul for yet another rotation.

Because I've been working overseas for so many years, being away from friends and family never really bothered me much; the absence became the new norm. However, once I started dating Kelly and we got engaged, my perspective changed. My time away felt a bit harder, but I also realized that working overseas would allow me to provide a comfortable life for my family—though I sometimes wondered how it would be later on down the line. But I've been extremely lucky because if there is anything I've learned, it's the value of support and working together.

Kelly and I have discussed what's next and know that the sacrifices we make now will pay off in the end. I expect to retire by the time I'm fifty-five and to be in a position to stay home, take care of the house and the kids, and give Kelly the opportunity to focus on her career. Having a game plan and an end date to the craziness makes things more bearable and puts us in a position to focus on the tasks at hand. It doesn't mean life is any easier, but it creates a foundation to do what needs to be done both at home and overseas. I have always believed that nothing is free and hard work always pays off in the end. Sure, the world throws you a kick in the nuts every now and again, but what doesn't kill you only makes you stronger.

Life at the embassy is actually pretty sweet for a direct-hire employee. As a senior Foreign Service officer, I live in my own studio apartment. Recently I was given an option to move into a one-bedroom unit, but I'm happy with my studio. There is 24/7 access to four full gyms, two swimming pools, a tennis court, and my favorite: an outside CrossFit gym. If you run as much as I do, there are several different courses around the embassy, and it's not uncommon to compete in multiple 5K runs and even a marathon.

The food is another perk with access to three full dining facilities that serve breakfast, lunch, and dinner along with a short-order grill that operates seven days a week. There are full holiday feasts and brunches on Friday and Saturday. You can eat as healthy or unhealthy as you want. There's also a concierge service where you can order groceries and food from town and send out your laundry to be dry-cleaned if needed.

My work routine is highly regimented. I usually work seven days a week, about ten to twelve hours a day. Depending on how many guys we have on ground, we're able to schedule a day off at least once a month, but honestly there isn't much to do on the embassy compound other than eat, work out, and sleep. My day consists of security briefings, random taskers, and putting out all kinds of fires, from people getting stuck in elevators and medical 911 calls to embassy fire dispatch, the occasional stolen laundry complaint, and terrorist attacks out in town. The operations center where I work is the brain of the embassy; every single call comes through us and my guys are shit hot when it comes to crisis management.

In Kabul, weekends are designated to be Friday and Saturday with Friday being the main day off for most embassy staffers. Since I fall under the security umbrella, they are pretty much just another work day for me. The rest of the embassy use weekends to let loose and party. Since we have two full liquor stores on the compound, I can safely say that drunken craziness does occur here.

Batshit craziness aside, living at the embassy is not that bad as long as you have a routine, and I stick to mine, making life pretty normal and the time go by fast. I typically get up about 0400, slam a pre-workout, and hit the CrossFit gym for an hour or two. Then I head back to my room, shower, go eat breakfast, call Kelly, and head to work. At work, no day is exactly the same. It can go from 0 to 100 in a split second and then BAM! back down to 0, leaving you feeling like you've been hit by a truck.

One nice thing about having a reliable, semi-normal schedule is that on most days I'm done by 1800 or 1900 and get back to my room at a civilized time to eat dinner. This means on a real plate with silverware rather than paper and a plastic fork at my desk. And best of all, I get a chance to read for a little bit before I go to bed.

My average work rotation runs 90/30, which means I rotate home for a thirty-day break and return to Kabul for ninety. When you break it down, I average about ninety vacation days—ninety days at home—per year. I have no work responsibilities and get paid for my time home. I won't say it's a true vacation, since I spend most of my time working around the house playing catch-up, but in the end, I am home with my family and that is all that matters to me.

While in Kabul, I'm grateful to have plenty of time to keep in touch with my family, and I talk to Kelly at least twice a day. Skype is our preferred way to communicate because I can see her rather than talk on the phone. Either way, she'll hang up when we argue, which isn't very often. Usually it's over something minor like when Brett misbehaves and I don't agree with how he was disciplined. But hey, that's just parenting. Kelly is good at telling me when he does something wrong, and over the years I've learned to sit back and let it all sink in before I explode—or not. This has not only helped me become a better parent but also to come up with more effective punishments.

A good example is when Brett broke the steel cable to the winch on our four-wheeler when he tried to tow the truck in the field. Kelly broke the news by asking me not to get mad while she showed me the broken cable on Skype. Since Brett was at school I couldn't yell at him, so I slept on it. The next day I just laid it all out about common physics and how it was impossible to pull a 2500 lb. truck with a 350 lb. four-wheeler using a winch with a cable rated to pull about 200 lbs. This was way more effective than flying off the handle and threating to end his life. In the end, his punishment fit the crime: He was banned from riding his bike until I came home and had to pay to get the cable fixed. Parents 1, Boy 0.

If there is one thing I've learned from my stepson, it's that what worked on me as a child does not work on him; as time changes, so must parenting. And it gets more complicated the more children you have because each kid is different. I always try to be fair with Brett and never hold a grudge. Once a punishment is handed out, you have to move on and keep rolling. For the last seven years, whenever I'm home, Brett and I go to breakfast every Tuesday. It's become a tradition. In general, like most teenagers, he hates to get up in the morning. But I do find it amazing how every other day of the week he barely makes the school bus but on breakfast Tuesdays the kid is twenty minutes early. You can't make this shit up!

Since being in Kabul for the last four years, I managed to finish my master's degree and just wrapped up a second bachelor's degree, so even with a tough work schedule there is plenty of free time to do what you want. My main focus, though, is training for races. And since the altitude here is over 6000 , I've taken my training to a higher level so that when I return home and compete, I have an advantage. The key is to schedule my leaves so that I'm home for no more than four or five days before my first race. My target for this upcoming rotation was the 7th annual World's Toughest Mudder. Since my first race in 2013, I would be competing for the fourth time. And because the event was moved to Georgia, I'd be experiencing a different venue as well. I was very excited about the new course and obstacles.

One of my better job perks is flexibility in when I can take leave. We just need to make sure that the needs of the operations center will be covered. With the exception of a family emergency, we rotate major holidays so you get July 4th, Thanksgiving, and Christmas/New Year's off every other year. This year I'd get Thanksgiving and next year after the baby arrived, I would get the other three. This was great as long as everything went according to plan, but we all know how that usually goes.

Kelly's original due date was January 19, 2019, which was perfect since I'd be home for Thanksgiving and then go back to work until January 10, giving me a week before the baby was due. Then the doctor announces that the baby will more likely arrive on January 12, so I changed my return to January 1— thanks to my good friend Bob and his willingness to trade some leave. Kelly and I also felt I should be home for eight weeks after the birth, and so the plan was for me to take medical leave from January 1 to March 6. As long as everything stayed on track, it should be the perfect schedule. So with the due date in hand, I submitted my request to Human Recourses and was given my tickets and a "Good to go." I would like to go on record as confirming that everything went according to plan, but as you might have guessed, that's not how it went.

CHAPTER 6

Turkey Day and Home Birth Blues

....

GROWING UP, holidays were always a big deal in my house, and it was the same for my wife. But until we moved to our home in Hampton, Connecticut, in 2016, holiday hosting was hard to do since we lived in a condo. And though I wouldn't be home for Christmas and New Year's, this would be my first Thanksgiving at the new place, and I was really looking forward to it. My favorite room is the dining room. It wasn't part of the original house—built in the 1700s—but it was part of the first addition built around 1800.

Hampton is a small town of about 2,000 people and 25.5 square miles. It wasn't incorporated until 1786. It boasts the oldest church in the state, built in 1754 and still in use, and a house built by Sally Bowers in 1776, known as "The House the Women Built," preserved here as well. According to Wikipedia, the cofounder of Annie's Homegrown and the inventor of Smartfood were from Hampton.

When Kelly and I committed to moving from the condo, we started looking for a historic home with ten acres or more of land. Over the course of three years, Kelly researched dozens of homes, but nothing really caught her eye. The one we finally found was the last house we looked at while I was home on that rotation, only two days before I went back to Afghanistan. I remember pulling into the driveway and walking around the yard, telling Kelly that if the inside is as nice as the outside, we may have found our new home. Once inside, Kelly went to work with a flashlight, crawling in and out of the basement and other nooks while dragging Bill, our real estate agent, alongside her. I sort of wandered around noting the cracks and sags and thinking of the electrical, plumbing, septic, and foundation codes. If you buy a home built in the 1700s, let's just say the chances of it being perfectly level are slim to none.

As I walked through the dining room I wondered about its history. When I caught up with Kelly in the living room, we were like, "Wow, this is it!" and made an offer pretty much on the spot. The house sat on five acres with an option to buy the adjoining 25-acre lot. After a discussion with the owners we did just that, and have been the proud owners of a centuries-old homestead on thirty acres of land since 2016.

When we closed on the house in August 2016, I had just stared my new job with the State Department and missed all the holidays, so 2018 would be my first Thanksgiving there, and I wanted to do it up right. It was also my first "big boy" experience of hosting a big family function, so instead inviting twenty-five people, which would have been easy to do, we decided to keep it at a dozen—still plenty of work but very manageable and a lot more fun.

Thanksgiving was especially good this year because my mom was able to make it. In each of the last fourteen years I would buy her a plane ticket so she could spend Thanksgiving with her sisters in Florida. Some years I joined her and even took Kelly and Brett along. This year we switched it up: Mom would go to Florida for Christmas and spend Thanksgiving with us.

Since I wouldn't be coming back home until right before Kelly's due date, I planned to spend most of November at home, which also meant I could compete in the 2018 World's Toughest Mudder in Georgia. I was taking Brett with me because it would give us an opportunity to bond, and I needed a pit crew member to help me out on the course. I don't think he realized how much work it would be, but since his grades were good, I allowed him to take a few days off from school. I also wanted to show him that no matter how old you are, the human body and mind are capable of tremendous feats—even at the point of physical and mental exhaustion, you can still keep going.

When it comes to traveling, I like to consider myself an expert. Having spent fifteen years in the military, I'd become an extreme planner, but I think it drives my family a little nuts. Kelly does keep reminding me that once the baby comes, I might as well throw all that shit out the window because I'll be on their time. But that's for then, and this is now. I got the WTM trip dialed in and made sure to book an early arrival in case of delay so no matter what, I could still get some rest prior to the race.

I pretty much dragged Brett out of bed before dawn for our 9:30 flight, got to the airport with time to spare, enjoyed some breakfast, and took off. The rest of the trip went smoothly—good thing, too, because the Mudder is a monster.

The World's Toughest Mudder is more or less the Super Bowl of obstacle course racing. It consists of a five-mile track plus twenty obstacles and you have twenty-four hours to complete as many laps as you can. As I mentioned earlier, this would be my fourth time competing, and every year I not only learn more

THE OLD DAD   33

and more about what works and what doesn't but also that each year seems to be colder than the previous one; this year would be no exception. Now there are some who believe that the Spartan World Championship is the premier event of obstacle course racing, and I won't argue the point. I run them all but consider the WTM to be the most difficult. And for the record, the elite athletes who compete in the Spartan races all compete at WTM as well.

My pre-race routine was typical: checking in, setting up the pit area, grocery shopping, eating, getting as much rest as possible, and, most importantly, watching The Weather Channel. Being from the northeast I figured the weather in Georgia in November would be a breeze—I mean, aren't we close to FL? But it wasn't to be. A cold front was coming in with rain and ice, so I knew it would be miserable. So my main goal was to make sure my pit area was as comfortable and dry as possible and Brett came through. And so off I went. With the exception of ice forming on my wetsuit, I was relatively warm as long as I kept moving and making time to stop in the pit area to fuel up and sometimes change out shoes and socks. This year nothing was able to stay dry, and by the next lap everything just frozen solid. Despite it all, I beat my previous race record of fifty-five miles, and if all goes well, I will compete in the 2020 World's Toughest Mudder with hopes of breaking my record yet again.

It was great having Brett with me. I really hope it was a learning experience for him and that he understands that running these types of races is a lot like life—you get out of it what you put into it. If you want to succeed at anything, it usually takes hard work and a little luck, but in the end all that dedication and sacrifice will pay off. Once we got home, it was back to business with a baby coming, and there was no changing that. I just hoped it stuck to the due date.

My favorite thing about the dining room is the fireplace. When it's fired up while we're eating dinner you can truly feel the history of the house and it helps me to appreciate the simple things in life. I sometimes think about all the past holidays spent in the dining room and two things come to mind: One is the true history of the house itself and the other is, *Holy shit, I hope this house isn't haunted!*

My wife and I joke that with a house this old, you can be sure that at some point someone died in it. I usually just laugh it off, but my wife has reported a couple of incidents, and I had one as well, right after we bought the house. I had just gotten back from Afghanistan. It was my one and only experience with what people call "the supernatural."

Kelly and Brett were at the store, and I was working on the office when our dog Clarice runs into the office, jumps into my lap, and tries to hide. It took a couple of minutes to calm her down, and since she weighs about fifty pounds, I had her jump off. I could still tell that something had spooked the shit out of her. Once off my lap, she sat by my side for a few more minutes and then lay down on the rug in front of my desk. I swear that no more than a few seconds went by and Clarice stood up with all her hair on end and started growling directly up at the ceiling. This freaked me out because she's the most laid-back dog I have ever met. I think what threw me off the most was that she kept backing up until she was leaning against my legs and then stood her ground. It sure looked like she was being protective, but of what, I had no clue.

As I said earlier, I'm not a big drinker. But all this went down just as I had finished pouring my second double IPA. A good double IPA is about 9% alcohol, and so when you go three months without any alcohol, a second hit makes me feel nice and relaxed. And then this, which got me thinking about ghosts. It hit all the main trip wires of a haunting or a paranormal incident based on what I remembered from TV and the internet; at least according to my IPA.

Even though I have memory issues because of my TBI, I somehow remembered that if you confront paranormal activity directly and show it that you aren't scared and want it to leave, it will unless it's demonic like in *The Exorcist*. So in true warrior fashion, I go out to my garage, grab a five-gallon jug of gas, and march back into my office. I placed the jug of gas on the floor and had a five-minute conversation with whatever was freaking my dog out. I don't remember my exact words, but it was something like, If you don't leave me or my family alone, I will burn this house to the ground and walk out of this place butt-naked so you can't attach yourself to anything of mine. And just to show I wasn't joking, I went downstairs and grabbed a lighter. After another ten minutes, I asked if I had made myself clear and were we going to have any problems. I took the silence as an "all clear" and calmly took the gas jug out of the house and put everything back in place. I opened up a few windows to get the gas smell out of the office before my wife got home; if I hadn't, a ghost would have been the least of my worries. To this day there have been no other issues as far as I can tell with paranormal activity. Living People – 1, Ghost – 0. (Though if I include Kelly's two incidents, it's Living People – 1, Ghost – 2.)

With a successful "first family Thanksgiving" under my belt, I was feeling pretty relaxed, but then I started worrying because the next time I'd be home, the baby would be on its way. Should I try one more time to talk Kelly out of her home birth obsession? If yes, I only had a few days, so I went to work. Right after Thanksgiving we had another visit with Janet, and this time she went over the final details of everything we needed to do and I realized I had put most of it off. Fortunately, according to Janet, Kelly was looking good, and pending any major concerns from the doctor, we were still cleared for a home birth delivery.

Feeling like my back was against the wall, I decided to take a more direct approach with Kelly and told her I didn't want anything to do with a home birth. Let's just say it was not a smart approach. We hardly ever argue, but this turned into a big ordeal, and I was told in not so many words that I wasn't going to win this battle. I did come to an understanding with myself that while being married is about finding mutual agreement, in the end you have to pick your battles and this wasn't one of them. Kelly continued to hold up her part of the bargain, and it kind of came down to me not wanting to fill up an inflatable tub in my living room in January.

My last week at home was spent buttoning up the house for winter, which also meant stocking up with wood and oil for heat. Kelly was knee deep in the fall semester of school and Brett was looking into high schools for his freshman year. So at this point, there was balance in the universe and all we had to do was wait for the baby.

We still hadn't agreed on a name. I wanted a more traditional name while Kelly was thinking of something more unique, and we didn't know if it would be a boy and or girl. We did decide that if we had a son, we wouldn't name him after me. I didn't really want another Vincent in the family and my brother Chris told me that when his son was born in October, he would name him Vincent. So at least that much was handled; now back to Afghanistan.

CHAPTER 7

Let's Stick to the Plan

······································

THE TRIP TO KABUL was smooth, and soon I was back in my typical routine. Kelly was about eight weeks from her due date and busting at the seams. To say I was a little nervous would be an understatement because I couldn't stop thinking of every worst-case scenario that could happen. But her meeting with the midwife the day I left was reassuring and tomorrow she'd be seeing her doctor. Everything was still looking good, but I was anxious.

Being 7,000 miles away there was nothing I could really do other than talk to Kelly a couple times a day and hope that Brett behaved so she could relax as much as possible. But she was getting ready for finals, and I knew it would be stressful for her. On the upside, her parents live less than an hour from our house and her brother and mother were helping out as much as possible, especially when it came to Brett. January 1 couldn't come soon enough.

The smartest thing I could do at this point was to dive back into work, and since I'd be leaving in five weeks, I decided to take the night shift from 6 p.m. to 6 a.m. That way, given the time difference back home, Kelly could just call me anytime if something popped up, and I'd be there. In the meantime, I was about four months from completing a second bachelor's degree so my free time was taken up with studying and increasing my CrossFit training to stay on track for upcoming races in 2019.

So up until now, I've kept saying that everything is going according to plan, but that ship changed ports on Friday, December 7, 2018. That day started normally enough. I talked to Kelly and she was getting ready to head to the doctor's office for her anatomy scan. She still hadn't gained enough weight, and so they scanned her about every two weeks to monitor the baby. All of her vital signs were great, and there was no cause for alarm other than her feeling really tired, which was pretty natural for a pregnant woman at this stage of pregnancy.

However, on Thursday Kelly had met with Janet, the midwife, who was concerned because Kelly mentioned that the baby wasn't as active as it had been over the last couple of months. But given that everything else was checking out and her doctor's appointment was the next day, we cautiously agreed to wait for further information. If something did come up and she started to feel any worse, she would go to the Emergency Room.

The next morning, she told me she felt about the same as the day before and was looking forward to her 2 p.m. appointment. Brett usually gets home about three, so I planned on calling the house after five so I could talk to Brett and see how things went. For me it was a typical Friday night shift, which are usually slow with the exception of the occasional fire alarm or drunken Foreign Service Officer. None of that was happening tonight, so it was especially boring and in Kabul, boring is a very good thing. When I called the house, Brett picked up and told me that Kelly wasn't home yet, so we chatted for a while and I told him I'd call back in a little bit.

On night shift I always go back to my room at 2 a.m. to make some espresso. When I got there, I checked my phone and noticed I had three missed calls and several IM's. They all said for me to call home ASAP and BAM! in an instant my day went from totally normal to panic mode. I immediately called and Brett picked up, telling me Kelly was going into surgery and Gram (Cindy, my mother-in-law) was coming to pick him up. I started to ask more questions, but he didn't have a lot of information. I told him not to worry, to stay calm, that Gram was on her way, and I was going to call her. I gave him the direct numbers to both my work phone and room extension because I had to get back to the operations center, and because it's a classified compartment, I'm not allowed to bring in my personal cell phone.

I first called Cindy. She told said she was still about forty minutes from picking up Brett and that the baby's heart rate had dropped so low that they had to do an emergency C-section. Apparently Kelly was fine, but no one was sure about the baby. My sister-in-law Amber was heading to the hospital so at least someone would be with Kelly. I told Cindy that Brett had both my numbers, and I would start making plans to come home as soon as possible.

I had never felt so helpless. All I could do was wait for news, go back to work, and start drafting my travel dates to adjust for having to leave now rather than in three weeks. Since the tickets were already paid for, it was just a quick date change and peak holiday travel was still days away so I was good. I would get everything prepped in the morning for the staff when they came into work, and because we have a crew that covers emergency travel, I knew I could get out of Kabul ASAP.

At 3:30 a.m. I received a call from Amber letting me know that Kelly was out of surgery, everything went well, and both she and the baby were fine. But because the baby was born five weeks early, it was being treated in the ICU and about to be transported to the nearest NICU. Amber assured me that this was normal procedure for premature babies. Then she handed the phone to Kelly.

To hear her voice was a huge relief. The last time we talked, she was on her way to a regular checkup. The first thing I asked was how she felt. She said she was fine but tired so I told her to get some rest, and I'd call her the next day when I would also know about my flight coming home. But first there were a few more details of what happened.

The reason for the emergency C-section, she explained, was because the baby had a low heart rate and a potentially constricted umbilical cord. The baby really was fine, she said, with all of its fingers and toes. Apparently for being five weeks premature, it was in excellent health. They were transporting the baby to the NICU at the Manchester, Connecticut, hospital and Kelly would join it later that night or first thing in the morning. Then she asked me if I wanted to know if it was a boy or a girl. I was so overwhelmed, that little detail had completely slipped my mind! She told me we had a boy and that, WOW! she was more surprised than me since from day one we assumed it would be a girl. And just like that, I was a father to a baby boy. I can't tell you the pure happiness I felt. Of course, I would have had just as much joy if I had a daughter, but a son, it was just so unexpected.

After hanging up the phone I just sat in pure silence, overwhelmed (again!) by emotions I had never felt before. In that moment I felt complete, as if I had mastered the world. More importantly, I felt truly blessed and very fortunate not only to have survived getting blown up in Pakistan but for all my accomplishments and how they had led up to this very moment. I have always had a strong sense of faith, but this was truly special.

After my call with Kelly I went back to work, a little unfocused but capable enough to finish the two hours left on my shift. I informed all the guys in the operations center and everyone was happy for me and some of them told me how much they love being a father and to enjoy while I can because before you know it, they are all grown-up. That put things in perspective because at forty-five years old, how much of his adulthood will I actually be able to enjoy?

Needless to say, there was no way in hell I was going to go to bed, so after turnover I grabbed some breakfast, went to the gym, and had one of my all-time best workouts. I was so full of energy I amazed myself. After my workout I went back to my room, showered, and tried to sleep. The last thing I did before finally nodding out was pray to God that Kelly would heal up fast and my son would continue to get stronger. I asked God to take whatever he needed from me—even my life—and give it to my son. And then I passed out from pure exhaustion.

After a three-hour power nap I was wide awake. Since I still had a few hours before heading back to work, I decided to check my email to see if there was any more news and there was not. One thing I've learned over all my years in the military is that no news is good news. I did find out that I would fly out of Kabul on Monday, December 10, and be home the next day. I was thinking that since both Kelly and the baby were fine, this would work fine. Then I got a text from Kelly asking if I was up and free to chat.

Since I couldn't wait to talk to her, I called right back just to hear her voice. She said the doctors had been great and had given her a full update about the baby's safe arrival at the NICU. The delivery had happened so fast that Kelly held the baby for maybe two minutes before he was put into the incubator and only got to see him for another five minutes before the ambulance showed up, so she was more than ready to be with him. She said she felt like she'd been hit by a truck and I could only imagine since Kelly is a pretty tough chick.

As Kelly and I talked about what happened, I realized how lucky we were. When Kelly had her appointment on Friday, the anatomy scan barely picked up a heartbeat. About five minutes after getting hooked up to the ER monitor, the nurses and doctors came running in and said the baby needed to come out now. Kelly had barely enough time to call her mother and that was it. They prepped her for the C-section and rushed her into surgery. Apparently, as the baby began to reposition itself, the umbilical cord stopped stretching and remained in a coil. As the baby grew, the cord became more and more restricted. But it was happening at such a slow pace that it was never detected. It was only discovered because Kelly was having bi-weekly anatomy scans; if it wasn't for that, we wouldn't have found out until it was too late. Modern Medicine – 1, Home Birth – 0.

After finding all of this out, I was shocked and felt even more blessed that our child had been saved. As a former medic, I still knew that he wasn't out of the woods yet, but he would get the best care needed in the NICU. Since I still had a day before departing Kabul, I decided to finish my last shift in the Operations Center. I didn't have to, but decided it would be more constructive to be at work with my friends than bouncing off the walls in my room waiting until it was time to start my journey home.

I landed at Bradley International Airport right on time, linked up with the car service for the ride back to the house, and soon enough was walking through my front door. I was so relieved to be back, but there was no time to relax. I spent a few minutes with Cindy, Brett, and the dogs, took a shower, found some clean clothes and had some food, then took off for the forty-five-minute drive to the hospital.

I was nervous and scared but also excited—a lot had happened over the last few days. After going through three layers of security to get to the NICU, I can assure you that if you are ever worried about someone stealing a baby from the hospital, these new security standards make it a very difficult thing to do, especially in the NICU.

When I got to the nurses' station and asked for Kelly's room number, all the nurses just smiled; it seemed that everyone was excited for me to see my son. When I got to her room the door was closed, so I knocked. I heard a familiar voice say, "Come in." She was using a breast pump so the nurses closed the room curtains and door. I opened up the curtain, said my usual "Hey, what's up?" and gave Kelly the biggest hug I could without putting too much pressure on her because I didn't really know how she was feeling. She didn't care one bit and squeezed me tighter than ever. I can't explain how great it felt to see my wife again.

After holding each other for a few minutes, I broke contact to use the bathroom. I think she might have been more excited than me to finally meet my son. I sat down on the bed and she filled me in on all the details. She said he was still hooked up to monitors and a feeding tube and not to freak out. So far, all the tests they did came back normal and he just needed to learn how to feed both by bottle and breast and, more importantly, put on a few pounds before he could be discharged. Since he was only 3 lbs. 13 oz., his body was still growing and needed to be in the incubator until he could self-regulate his body temperature. We decided on his name so it was now official: Collin Vincent Capodicci, born December 7, 2018, at 18:17. And now it was time to meet my son.

The walk from Kelly's room to the NICU wasn't very long, but it felt like eternity. I didn't know what I expected to see other than a tiny little baby with all sorts of wires and tubes attached to it, but that wasn't the case. A nurse met us at the door, briefed me on NICU etiquette such as washing your hands with a surgical scrub for three minutes when you come into the NICU from the outside and also when you leave and to use a hand sanitizer while you are in the ward. Nothing too crazy but some good common sense given the health risks of all the babies in the NICU, not just yours.

After drying my hands, Kelly walked me into the NICU, and there he was, all bundled up and asleep in the incubator. I've seen a lot of awesome things in my life but seeing my son for the first time was hard to beat, and it brought tears to my eyes. Since it was time for him to eat, Kelly and the nurse started prepping his bottle. They first had him feed from Kelly's breast, followed by the bottle and then the feeding tube to make sure he took in his minimum amount of milk: three ounces every three hours until he reached about five pounds.

After he finished feeding, I got to hold him for the very first time. I never realized how tiny and fragile a 3 lb. 13 oz. baby actually is. Kelly called him her little hamster, and I referred to him as a tiny old man because as a "preemie" he had no fat on him. I also told Kelly he has the new baby smell, which for some reason no one found funny. I tend to use humor when I'm emotional, and sitting there holding Collin for the first time was a very sobering moment with emotions I'd never felt before. Maybe it's just a military thing.

About forty-five minutes later, I got to meet the doctors and nurses and thank them for the great care both Kelly and Collin had received so far. All in all, Collin was where you would want and expect a five-week preemie to be: he needed to put on about two to three pounds, take breast milk or the bottle for a full feeding, pass the car seat test, and regulate his own body temperature. We still had a lot of work ahead of us, but he was stable and in good hands which put both of us at ease. And now that I was home, they would discharge Kelly.

It was past 10 p.m. before we got home and we were spent. I helped Kelly get situated, and she was soon asleep. I wanted to watch TV for a while because I didn't feel tired even after being up for twenty-seven hours, but as soon as I put the recliner back and the dogs jumped on my lap, I must have passed out because the next thing I knew it was almost midnight. This would pretty much be my new norm for the next few weeks until Collin was released, so let the games begin.

CHAPTER 8

Christmas at the NICU

RETURNING HOME from Afghanistan is usually a relaxing time as my transition from being overseas to the good ol' US is a chance to get back into the stateside grove. But when you have a premature baby in the NICU, all I can say is, "Relax? What is that?" I mean it sure was nice to sleep in my own bed and to see my wife, but since Collin was still in the NICU, neither Kelly nor I could really enjoy being home. We wanted our son to be there with us.

Since Kelly was going to breastfeed Collin, she had to start using a breast pump regularly. In this way she could get used to producing milk regularly and also pump milk to bring to the NICU every day when visiting with Collin. And so after nodding off in the recliner, I joined Kelly in bed and immediately fell into a deep sleep. Not long after, Kelly woke me up in a fit because the hospital's breast pump stopped working. I got out of bed and tried to trouble-shoot but the damn pump just wouldn't work. So now I'm thinking that it's no big deal to just get another one in the morning. What I didn't know is that Kelly needed to pump regularly so that one the breasts didn't stop producing milk and, more importantly, because as a breast fills with milk, it becomes painful. This I learned in a few short, stressful minutes from Kelly, which meant waiting for a new breast pump was no longer an option. So here I am, a little after midnight, trying to find some place that wasn't only open but also had a breast pump. Fortunately we have modern technology, and a quick internet search on my phone showed that Walmart was open 24/7 for the Christmas season and literally had twenty different breast pumps.

A twenty-five-minute drive to Walmart put me in the breast pump aisle, but then I had to figure out which one Kelly needed. I go back on my iPhone to learn about breast pumps and thirty minutes later am as close to a breast pump expert as I'll ever get but still don't know what to do. I finally give up and buy the best pump money can buy and BAM! $210 later I'm back in my car headed for home. Mission accomplished!

Back at the house we spend about thirty minutes figuring the pump out, and as soon as Kelly starts pumping milk—it's now 2 a.m.—I close my eyes and the next thing I know it's 7 a.m. Kelly was already up and pumping again to make sure she had a good amount to take to the hospital. She called the hospital and Collin was fine, so she decided to sleep in. I took care of the dogs, ate some breakfast, and went to the gym because that's what I do. CrossFit has been my escape for a few years now and has become a ritual I really enjoy.

Cindy took Brett and the dogs to her house so Kelly and I could focus on Collin and the hospital. Due to her surgery, Kelly wasn't allowed to drive until cleared by her doctor, so for the next few days I would drive to the hospital in the afternoon and stay until Collin had dinner. The drive to the hospital was forty-five minutes exactly, and over the next three weeks we made that trip every day.

Collin was still being fed every three hours, and twenty minutes prior to each feeding we would change him. After each feeding he would sleep until the next one. Kelly and I switched back and forth between feeding and changing him because I needed to get comfortable with the changing part. As for Kelly, she was locked in with Collin from day one—no big deal. Have I said she's an amazing wife and mother? I, on the other hand, was scared shitless because he was so tiny, and I didn't know quite how to hold him. Kelly changed him in like two minutes; it took me ten.

Since Collin was doing remarkably well, we were able to hold him more and more while he slept. Kelly and I would hand him off to each other throughout the day, though I still felt a little uncomfortable if Kelly or the nurse weren't in the room. But I knew it was something that sooner or later I would have to do, so I jumped right in and it became easier and easier. I even got more efficient at changing his diapers and feeding him. Between the bottle and the feeding tube, he was finally starting to put on some weight. He wasn't out of the clear yet, but at this rate of improvement we would likely bring him home in a couple of weeks. The big benchmarks were Collin getting over four pounds and passing the car seat test.

On December 13, Kelly met with her doctors to check on her healing and find out when she'd be clear to drive again. The appointment was a "good to go"; she was cleared to drive. Now we could double-team hospital duty so one of us was always with Collin throughout the day, from when he got up in the morning until he finally went to sleep at night. Kelly would get up with me in the morning at about 5:30 and leave the house by 6:30 or 7:00 so she could get there in time for morning rounds to get up to speed on how Collin did that night.

As for me, I'd make sure Brett got off to school, the dogs were fed, and take care of any house chores that needed to be done. I would than head out for a morning CrossFit class that would still give me plenty of time to take care of anything else that came up. Most of the time it was meal prepping and taking care of the dogs; I kept busy but not to the point where I was ever overwhelmed. At about 2:30, I would head to the hospital to spend some time with both Collin and Kelly before she would pass him to me and head home to get Brett off the bus and make sure he was fed and didn't burn the house down, which for some reason has always been a concern for me. Maybe it had to do with all the years of my parents telling me to watch my brothers because they might burn down the house.

After Kelly left, I would feed Collin, put him back in the incubator, then go to the lounge and eat the dinner I brought from home. If he was still sleeping after dinner, I would usually do some school work or read until he got up. I enjoyed those first few minutes when he woke up because he was still a little groggy and a lot easier to change. I'd then put him in a fresh set of pj's and feed him. The more I did all this, the easier it got, but I always hated forcing his jammies over his soft little head, so I usually ended up stretching the hell out of them to make the hole bigger. You could say I pretty much ripped up all of them.

After a few days the routine became pretty normal, and it gave Kelly an opportunity to stick to a good sleeping schedule. Once we brought Collin home, we would be on his schedule and sleep would be a luxury. Both of us worked really well together. I thought of it like a NASCAR pit crew: as Kelly would prep Collin's bottle or feeding tube, I would change him or we'd switch roles. Since I had eight weeks off from work, it was nice to be able to help Kelly out like this, but I was nervous about going back to work when the time came.

Over the course of the first week, Collin got stronger and you could see him develop more and more. They even tried to remove his feeding tube, which we didn't think he was ready for, and sure enough they put it back twenty-four hours later. But a week after that he just pulled the damn thing out himself and that was almost it for the feeding tube—they still used it every two to three hours but with less and less volume. It was great to follow his progress.

It was hard for people to visit Collin in the NICU, but my mother Jerri was one of the exceptions. I made the two-hour trip to Bridgeport to pick her up so she could see him, which worked out great since she was spending Christmas in Florida with her sisters and I was able to give her a ride to the airport the next morning. It also worked out because the following week, I picked her back up so she could spend even more time with Collin.

The only issue that came up was whether I should stay after Collin ate dinner. At that point I would usually leave the NICU to come home because Collin would go right to sleep, but Kelly was worried because there was no one with him. If I stayed and watched him sleep and I would fall asleep myself, so what was the point? He had 24/7 care so I wasn't worried about him and honestly didn't think he would really notice. If there were problems I would have definitely slept there, but he was making progress and didn't really need me then.

About halfway through his second week in the NICU, the doctors thought he might be ready to come home, which meant we would have him for Christmas Eve. Kelly and I weren't convinced, but the doctors thought he'd be fine and would make the call the next day. That afternoon when I went to the hospital to switch out with Kelly, I brought the car seat just in case. Little did I know that during his afternoon feeding, he had actually stopped breathing until the nurse gave him a slap on his ass to get him going again. They assured us that this was common in premature babies because they aren't developed enough to eat and breathe at the same time. Because of this, he had to stay an extra week in the hospital, which made Christmas out of the question, but New Year's Eve was still a possibility.

That night the car seat went back to the house, and we would spend Christmas Eve and Day at the NICU with Collin. We wanted to make sure that Brett would still have a good Christmas at the house with Kelly and me, and in true Heroic Mom fashion, Kelly came up with a plan that pretty much took care of everyone.

Christmas has always been huge with my family. My brother Chris has more or less taken over as Christmas Eve host, and since he's now married with a family, he carries the torch as the main location for all Christmas Eve activities. In the past, our family would host huge Christmas Eve parties with twenty to thirty guests who would stop by from early evening to well after midnight. That tradition continues to this day.

And so the plan was for Kelly and I to stick to our hospital routine and stop at my brother's house after we left the hospital. But I stayed for a bit after she left to feed Collin and read him *'Twas the Night Before Christmas*. That alone made it the best Christmas Eve ever and I will read it to him every Christmas for many years to come. Once I got home, Kelly was already in bed, out like a light, so I stayed up to watch *Die Hard: A Christmas Story*, which might become my new Christmas movie.

On Christmas Day, Kelly left the house early for the hospital. I took a morning run and then spent a couple of hours with both she and Collin. One thing I really liked about the NICU were the nurses, who were all very festive and decorated the NICU, making sure all the babies had Santa hats. I drove to Brett's grandparents' house to have dinner and then brought him home so we could all open gifts together. This year we opened them in the evening rather than the morning, but we still all spent Christmas together and that's what mattered. We did miss Collin.

Before we knew it, Christmas was over and it was time to focus on getting Collin healthy and bringing him home. His continued to improve, put on more weight, there were no more breathing incidents, and they finally removed his feeding tube. We'd been moving slowly and carefully and it sometimes felt like going backwards, but progress was being made.

CHAPTER 9

Bringing Home the Hamster

·······································

THE WEEK AFTER CHRISTMAS was pretty much the same as both Kelly and I stuck to our routine of spending as much time with Collin as possible. My mom was coming back from Florida this week so it worked out perfectly to pick her up at the airport and bring her to see Collin. Then it would be back to my house for the weekend. But that's not exactly how things went.

After picking her up at the airport, we swung by the hospital where she stayed with me for Collin's night feeding and putting him to bed, which I knew she would really enjoy. It also helped that in the ten days she was away, he'd gotten a little bigger. After putting Collin down, we went out to dinner. Since she'd been traveling all day, I knew she would be tired, so the plan was that she would spend the night at my house and then in the morning we'd swing back by the hospital and then I would take her back home.

This is where the wrench got thrown in. As we left the hospital, the doctor decided that it was time for Collin to come home and scheduled it for the next day, which was Saturday, December 29. Now the plan now was to bring my mom home early on the morning so that I could make it back to the house to pick up Kelly and get back to the hospital by 9 a.m. It was simple on paper except I'd have to leave my house at 4 a.m. to bring Mom home so everything else could happen. It was going to be another very long day.

As I headed back to the house after dropping Mom off, Kelly called and told me to come to the hospital because her car was making a weird sound and was no longer drivable. Okay, how much is *that* going to cost? After getting to the hospital, I took Kelly's car for a test drive and sure enough it needed to be towed. I swapped the car seat into my car and now I was finally ready to take my son home for good.

While Kelly was getting last-minute instructions from the doctor and scheduling follow-up appointments for Collin, I prepped the car seat and signed him out of the hospital. What I found amusing was the idea of signing for a human life. I laughed and told the nurse that I'd never done this before and it felt kind of funny. Maybe it's because I have a stranger-than-normal sense of humor, but in my line of work you have to.

Putting Collin in his car seat for the very first time was kind of nerve-racking and I had a hard time pulling it off. The nurses sat back and watched, and I'm sure they've experienced this comical event on a regular basis. But as long as I wasn't hurting the baby, they would let me figure it out. Kelly once again came to the rescue, and we laughed at how clumsy I was. With Collin signed out of the hospital and in the car seat, it was finally time to take him home. And while I was nervous, Kelly was acting like a professional.

The drive from the hospital felt a lot longer than usual because I had the most precious cargo in the world in my car and protecting him with my life was the only thing on my mind. I can't speak of past experience since Collin was my first child, but I'm pretty sure most new fathers have the same feeling. We finally pulled into the driveway, safe and sound, but this was only the beginning. I had no clue what would happen next.

My first mission was to collar the dogs to protect Collin from them accidentally jumping and hitting the car seat. Clarice was mostly mellow, but Winnie was still a puppy and a bit hyper. I gave Kelly the all clear and she brought Collin into the house and took him into the great room, where a wood stove had been keeping it nice and warm. Kelly took Collin out of his car seat and immediately gave him his bottle while I brought the dogs back in—but kept them out of the great room. Collin finished his bottle and went right to sleep, giving us time to start putting his stuff away and preparing his place upstairs. So far so good! I remember saying to myself that this didn't seem so bad since all he does is eat and sleep. The surprises were yet to come!

Collin still needed to be fed every two hours, and Kelly was still pumping breast milk. So far, the routine was pretty straightforward: we would wake him up, change him, and feed him, which took about forty-five minutes, and then 90% of the time he would go right back to sleep. But the thing to remember is the two-hour interval doesn't start again after he finishes his bottle; it starts from the time you wake him up, which leaves about an hour or so to get other stuff done around the house. It was no different at night, but if done right, we could wake him, change him, feed him, and get him back to sleep in thirty minutes or less, giving us an hour or more of sleep at a time. But if his eating was slow or he wasn't able to get a couple of good burps out, that hour-plus of sleep got a lot shorter before he needed to be woken up again.

Kelly, steadfast as always, would set her alarm for every two hours. Once it went off, we'd start the routine. She would wake Collin up while I got his bottle so that once I was back, he'd be changed and ready to feed while Kelly pumped. Since she was augmenting breast milk with formula, we would prep bottles ahead of time so that at any given time we'd have six to eight of them ready to go. That may seem like a lot, but when you're feeding every two hours, it goes quick.

For the first couple days our system worked, and I stopped worrying about how we would handle the two-hour feedings. But then all of a sudden, BAM! my lack of sleep caught up with me and knocked me sideways. Having served in the military and working overseas for so many years, I was no stranger to being tired. But this kind of tired was like nothing I'd ever felt before.

During the day Kelly was able to take short catnaps, but I had a deal with her: as long as Collin was taken care of and I had some free time, going to the gym would be up to me. So in my usual fashion, I gave up sleep to work out. In my twenties that wouldn't have been an issue, but doing it when you're forty-five catches up to you fast. I had reached a point where if I sat still for more than five minutes, I would pass out. Just ask Kelly. I can't tell you how many pictures she has of me slumped over while feeding Collin. But don't bust my chops for that—I had a pillow to prop up my arms, and as long as I was in the recliner or his rocker, there was never any threat of him being dropped.

We took Collin to a pediatrician about once a week. He was also having issues with holding down formula, so we had to take him to a GI specialist. It turned out he had an allergy too dairy, so now the mission was to find him the right type of formula. It took about two weeks of trial and error to find one he could tolerate with the breast milk. He was also having issues with acid reflux so we added a mild antacid liquid to his schedule that we would drip into his mouth with a syringe. For all of that, both Kelly and I felt extremely lucky that these were his only two major issues. Everything else was positive, and he was definitely making progress.

Having a newborn during the winter is challenging because flu season is in full swing but everyone wanted to see him. Kelly and I decided that other than our parents and a few family members, no one else was allowed and we would put off all social events until the spring—not that we had any time for such things. We also agreed that if you wanted to meet Collin, you needed to have a flu shot. Most people did, a few didn't, but in the end it was a good call because no feelings were hurt.

During the flu season our pediatrician ran a tight ship and I was impressed with how they cared for all of their patients. As soon as you showed up at the receptionist window, you were checked in and taken directly to see the doctor; sick kids had to wear a mask and were brought to a separate part of the clinic. On most days we were in and out in twenty minutes unless there were bigger issues that needed to be addressed.

Every week Collin seemed to make major improvements. Two weeks after bringing him home his weight had more than doubled to a little over eight pounds, which was still in the lower percentile but he was clearly making progress with the exception of a possible milk allergy. He was still feeding every two hours with a combination of formula and breast milk. (After Collin was born, Kelly had trouble pumping enough milk because of the amount he constantly needed. But over time she pumped less while formula was used more, and by early- to mid-February she stopped pumping and breast-feeding altogether and relied entirely on formula. This was a blessing since she was able to sleep a little more.) After a while, Kelly and I started to take turns feeding him so one of us could go back to bed. But by then day and night had kind of blended together, and I think I just went on autopilot. Looking back at it all, I still got off easy because I knew that sooner or later, I would go back to work and it would be Kelly doing it all.

Although I had no problems changing Collin's diapers, I did have trouble with his onesie, which he always had on since it was winter. Now anyone who's familiar with the onesie knows that it's a pretty straightforward operation, but maybe that's when you put it on a normal-sized baby. I mean, with regular one-piece pajama outfits, all you do is lay it down, put baby on top, slide arms in the little sleeves, buttoned the whole thing up, and mission accomplished—all dressed and ready to go. But those onesies were different.

Collin was still tiny, and every time I started to pull one over his head, I was afraid the pressure of it would give him brain damage because of his soft spot. I can't tell you the number of times I'd finally get him dressed and he'd immediately throw up or poop and have to be changed again. It was really demoralizing. But when you have a newborn, you learn soon enough that you no longer have control of anything and are pretty much at their service 24/7. What I know now and didn't know then is that it's pretty much impossible to break your baby putting on a onesie. Kelly always made it look easy, but that little outfit kicked my ass every time.

Speaking of poop stories, one night during the second week of Collin being home, Kelly woke me up out of a dead sleep. She said she needed my help and from the sound of her voice I knew it was serious. Sure enough, as I jumped out of my side of the bed, I saw that Kelly was elbow-deep in poop and Collin was covered in it. She cleaned him up and left to wash her hands while I did a final wipe and finished the diaper change. But Collin had other plans. When I tilted his legs up to slip in his diaper, BOOM! he let out a shit that to this day reminds me of stomping on a large tube of toothpaste. It not only got on my hand and arm but splattered on the sheets, the comforter, Kelly's pillow, and even managed to hit the headboard. *Holy shit, Kelly! I really need your help right now!* At first I thought she might be mad because I wasn't good at changing a diaper, but when she saw the carnage, she realized my cry for help was reasonable.

So we changed his diaper, put clean clothes on him, and then Kelly took him downstairs to eat so I could clean up and change the sheets. The next thing I know we're all back in bed so we could do it all over again. Fortunately the next feeding went according to plan, and as Kelly and Collin went back to sleep, I started my routine of dogs, Brett, breakfast, and the gym, thinking to myself, I'm too old for this.

CHAPTER 10

Sleep, What Is That?

···

I KNOW I'VE MENTIONED sleep deprivation many times over the last few chapters, but I would not be giving the phenomenon full justice if I didn't devote an entire chapter to it. I mean, we've all experienced a lack of sleep at different times in our life, but there are many forms of it that I've broken down into several types.

According to the experts on Google, getting enough sleep is kind of important. Most of the studies I found agreed that adults between the ages of eighteen and sixty need a minimum of seven hours of sleep a night. That being said, more than half of all adults in the US get less than that. Many studies also conclude that if you do get less than seven hours of sleep, you shouldn't go longer than seventeen hours without trying to catch up. Otherwise you're in danger of experiencing some sort of sleep deprivation. (Normal infants require twice as much sleep as adults.) How long can the average adult go without sleep? Apparently, the world record is 266 hours or about eleven days. Prior to this, a high school student from California in 1964 stayed awake for 264 hours. The report on this was very detailed, discussing how at the end of the experiment, the kid began to hallucinate until finally falling asleep. He fully recovered.

The lack of sleep can kill you, though. The longer you go without sleep, the more likely you are to die from an accident because sooner or later your body will start to shut down and force you to sleep. If I remember correctly, about 90,000 accidents a year are caused by sleep deprivation due to the driver falling asleep at the wheel, but actual deaths are less than a thousand.

There is also a very rare sleep disorder called Fatal Familial Insomnia (FFI) which can result in death. FFI is a gene disorder that impacts the part of the brain that regulates our sleep. FFI apparently has no cure, and most of the articles I read concluded that once the condition is triggered, death occurs within twelve to eighteen due to changes in body temperature, weight loss, and a lack of appetite that finally lead to dementia.

I decided to categorize all my experiences with lack of sleep according to certain times of my life such as my early teens, partying in college, military service, adult life, and bringing home a newborn. Like most people, I put sleep aside for such things as partying, sex, work, and studying and each one took its fair share out of me, but the "newborn lack of sleep" phase hands down beat all the others.

EARLY TEEN YEARS: This is a unique time in one's life because you are at a crossroad: your body still needs sleep to grow, but you really don't feel the need to sleep and would much rather have fun. This is a time where you usually have a part-time job, come home to do homework, and spend all night talking to your girlfriend until it's time to catch the bus. Throw in a video game or three and you can easily go a day or more without sleep. And since you don't possess the skill of proper time management, you can sometimes stay up until you literally pass out and your parents think you're sick or something.

During this period, I was actively involved in Boy Scouts, so when we would go on a weekend camping trip, I wouldn't sleep the entire weekend. At summer camp I would stay up late working on merit badge projects and sometimes hike twelve to fifteen miles on the Appalachian Trail, set up camp, stay up until 1 or 2 a.m., make breakfast a few hours later, and then hit the trail again without batting an eye.

COLLEGE. College life took lack of sleep to a whole new level because you were in one of two groups: those who stayed up all night to study or those who stayed up all night to party. This was also a unique time because you either learned about time management or got crushed by tests and deadlines. The best students figured out a way to do both: get good grades and party. You spend the first semester of your freshman year doing everything wrong and then slowly figure things out. It's a "sink or swim" time of your life.

When I was in high school, I wasn't very social person, but in college I did a complete one-eighty. I discovered partying and hooking up in my first two weeks and didn't really appreciate college until I was an adult, and by then it was clearly too late. I never figured out how to manage my sleep, so I would party like a rock star and then go to class until I was so exhausted I would sleep for about eighteen hours, wake up, and start all over again. I did it all wrong.

THE MILITARY. Lack of sleep went to yet another level in the military because you basically have no control if and when you actually get to sleep. It forces you to push your limits but also learn how to manage your free time. Just ask anyone who has gone thought any type of military training; they will tell you how miserable it was grabbing five-minute power naps a few times a day and then being expected to function at 100% because in certain situations, lives depended on your ability to do your job and not nodding off.

Like everything else, though, your body adjusts over time and before you know it, sleep deprivation is no longer an issue. After a full day of military training you go out and get hammered, roll right into formation in your gear, then run ten miles straight from the bar.

In the Navy I went through about every type of no-sleep scenario you can think of and was always able to do my job. Even during all my deployments overseas, my body adjusted pretty quickly to a lack of sleep. A normal day consisting of coming back from a mission as the sun came up, going through debriefing, prepping gear, eating, and then finally going to sleep just to get up three or five hours later to work out, eat, and brief for another mission. I have always been amazed on how fast my body adapted.

Once I left the military and started contracting and then later working for the State Department of State, my experiences with lack of sleep depended on where I was. When training or going through consultations in D.C., my schedule was the typical 9 to 5, which bored me rather quickly. But in Iraq, Pakistan, and Afghanistan, my sleep patterns were more typical of my time in the military, but my normal schedule usually consisted of 12- to 14-hour days.

I have come to the conclusion that my experience with lack of sleep helped mold me into the person I am today. It's easier for me to push myself and, more importantly, I'm in tune with my body. I know how to compensate for lack of sleep through diet adjusting my activity levels. It just made me a lot tougher all around.

THE COLLIN ERA. It may sound like I got all my sleep patterns figured out and I actually thought I had, but then Collin came into my life and sleep deprivation got real. Although I've taken my share of hits, Kelly has suffered the most and yet she continues to blow my mind with everything she's able to do, especially when I'm away at work. When I get back, I've got to adjust because balancing it all is truly exhausting. I'm conflicted because on the one hand, I love watching Collin's development and how he reacts to new experiences, but on the other, I can't wait for him to get a little older so he can eat and go to the bathroom on his own.

Harkening back to my military days, I did re-learn to take catnaps at the drop of a dime. I can't tell you how many times I sat down and as soon as my body started to relax, I would pass out—hard. I remember taking Brett to his teen weight-lighting class, and as I sat in a bean bag chair in the lobby, I slept for a solid forty-five minutes while he finished training and stretching out. It was kind of crazy to think that in order to get some sleep, I needed to be away from home. Fortunately for Kelly, she slept every time the baby did, and that's when I had time to help out around the house, take care of the dogs, fix dinner, and make sure Brett did all of his homework before he went to bed.

Collin was starting to hit all the weight goals the doctors set for him, which meant we would be able to go longer between feedings—from every two hours to every three hours at night. When Collin reached the magic number of ten pounds, Kelly no longer had to feed him every three hours at night. And if he slept all night, she would only have to feed him in the morning, but during the day it was still every two hours.

My biggest takeaway for all my years of sleep deprivation is your body can adjust to it if you develop a routine and a flow and some really good habits. To pull it off, it's essential to maintain your body and mind like a machine. From my years of experience, a key element is to maintain a consistent sleep schedule no matter how short or long the intervals. Also, get in the sun as much as possible, even if only for a few minutes and no matter what time of year it. Cut back on caffeine and find a balance. For me, I was good to go with a pre-workout coffee and a 2 p.m. espresso. Healthy eating is also a key factor because if you fill up with crappy foods such as cakes and pies, they will slow you down and you'll gain weight. I ate healthy and more frequently and was able to burn fuel more efficiently. Finally, my most important advice of all is to stay hydrated. Proper hydration helps to replenish your body tissues and, what most people don't realize, increases blood flow to the brain. So that's my list. They may not work for everyone, but I know they worked for me.

One thing's for certain: as your baby grows, your sleep deprivation will come to an end. Collin now sleeps solidly for six to nine hours every night, and I've become a ninja when walking around the house while Collin's asleep. Ask any father: the look you get from your wife if you wake it up after she finally puts a fussy baby down will guarantee a long night.

Now that Collin is sleeping regularly, I've begun to appreciate the value of a good night's sleep. After all my years overseas and suffering from that brain injury, getting a full night of sleep was next to impossible. But when I'm home with Collin, I sleep like a rock. I think it has a lot to do with how good it feels to spend time with my family and going through the process of being a new dad.

CHAPTER 11

Learning the Ropes

....

OVER THE YEARS of growing up and becoming an adult, I've had more and more responsibilities. This was especially true in both the military and as a civilian overseas due to having people's lives literally in my hand. When going into combat operations and knowing that it's no longer about me but the guys to the left and right of me, I had to do my job to keep them alive just as they were responsible for keeping me alive. When going out on missions, I was never worried about getting injured or even killed; I came to terms with all that after my first deployment. What scared me the most was not doing my job, failing the guys who relied on me. Needless to say, I took my job very seriously; most people will never experience that type of stress. So, when I found out Kelly was pregnant, I figured, "How bad could it be? It's not like someone's life depends on me." Wrong!

Now having a child is nothing like going to war, but when you break it down, you *are* responsible for another human being, not only to feed and care for it but to be a good mentor as it grows up. Because if the kid grows up to be a jerk, it's kind of my fault, which makes being a parent one hell of a learning experience for everyone. That freaked me out a little because war is relatively simple: your job is taking care of your buddies and bringing hate to the people who are trying to kill you.

I figured it would be somewhat less stressful because Kelly had already been a mom with Brett who was basically a good kid, but it turns out that each and every kid is different. What works for one will most likely not work for the other, and this was especially true with Collin. Strap yourself in! Since Collin was only a few months old, I figured I didn't have to change my habits because he can't comprehend certain things like rock music, war movies, and profanity. I mean, after spending all those years in the military and overseas, you can be sure that "Fuck" is a common word in my vocabulary. I assumed it would stay that way and I could concentrate on learning how to take care of him.

One of the first things I had to get used to was the constant washing of my hands since it was flu season. I felt like I was back in my Hospital Corpsman days working in the ER at Great Lakes Naval Hospital. Pet the dog, wash your hands. Go out to the garage, wash your hands. Pick up the phone, wash your hands. My hands became a chapped bloody mess! At first I thought that Kelly was overdoing it, but as time went on, I realized that it was a good idea since Collin was still developing from being a preemie and catching the flu could literally kill him.

Cleaning and filling bottles required a whole-system algorithm because you can't just throw some tap water in a bottle with a few scoops of powder formula, shake the shit out it, throw it in the microwave, and then stick it in the baby's mouth. You have to boil water and sterilize the bottle and nipples before putting them in a special rack to air dry. We did find these sterilizing bags you throw in the microwave, and they were awesome. They saved at least fifteen to twenty minutes each time, and when you go through up to ten bottles a day from feeding Collin every two hours, and it adds up. And time is precious, especially when lack of sleep is dogging you.

Once the bottle and nipples are dry and sterile, it's back to boiling water for mixing the formula. I felt like a damn chemist because we had to adjust the servings per ounce to make sure that Collin received roughly twenty-two calories per to both maintain his body weight and continue to put on more weight. Once that was done, we wrote the date and time they were filled and put them in the refrigerator in order from oldest to newest so we could just work our way backwards. They usually lasted until the next morning and so at lunchtime it was time to make the next batch.

I also discovered the importance of a good burping during feeding; the trick is figuring out when to stop the feed to burp the baby, because I learned the hard way that it's not a good idea to wait until they've finished an entire bottle. Kelly needed to take a shower and asked me to change and feed him. I took him downstairs, warmed up the bottle, turned on the TV, and sat in the rocker. No big deal, right? This was Collin's first feeding of the day and usually when he seemed the hungriest. He polished off half the bottle in about two minutes with no intention of stopping. I pulled it out of his mouth, put him over my shoulder, and started tapping his back lightly like I had done multiple times in the past. This time, though, he didn't want anything to do with that so a meltdown ensued. I figured since he wanted the bottle back, I'd let him have it and in a split second he went from crying to slamming down the remaining formula like it was crack or something.

We wrapped up the feeding and he started to fall back asleep so I figured, mission accomplished right? Hell no! Just as his eyes started to close, he let out a burp that sounded like Homer Simpson and began spitting up everything he had just taken in over me, the rocker, the rug, and even Clarice, our older dog. What I couldn't understand is how three ounces of milk turned into what seemed like a gallon. Collin seemed content after this, so I changed him out, put him in his little Moses basket, and started cleaning up puke before it stained the rug and the rocker material. My takeaways: dogs really love to eat vomit. Always clean the baby first. Clean up the surrounding areas next. Then clean yourself.

Changing Collin was another task I had to conquer. I started out thinking, "How hard could it be?" But once they get fidgety and start squirming around, things get complicated. One key thing when changing a diaper is to prep everything first: diapers, wipes, clothes, ointment, baby powder, and extras of everything because no sooner do you change them, they might do the deed again. *Hey Dad, where do you think you're going? I have a gift for you!*

Since Collin was born in January and being premature, making sure the house was warm during the day became another top priority, and that was pretty easy because we had a great stove in the main room. It did get cold at night, though since, well, the house was built in the 1700s. Thankfully he seemed to take after his mother and always felt warm, where I'm always cold. I think all my years in the military being wet, cold, and miserable plus having hypo and hyperthermia more than once most likely threw off my body's ability to regulate temperature. During the day we kept him in his winter pajamas and that worked very well. We did try to keep a little beanie hat on his head, but he wasn't a big fan. At night he wore the same outfit and had a light blanket that he usually threw off.

Since it was January and flu season, we only took him out when he had a doctor's appointment, but it was a chore because once he was dressed up, he looked like a cross between Maggie Simpson in her winter baby jacket and Randy from *A Christmas Story*. He literally was not able to move, which drove him crazy. Throw in the fact that we had to shoehorn him into a car seat and he never looked comfortable. I did finally get the hang of dressing him, though to this day I hate putting on his little T-shirts because you have to pull them over his head and then slide his arms through the sleeves and I always felt like I was going break something. Kelly, of course, was a pro at it.

As the weeks passed, our routines got better, which Kelly and I were grateful for. It took a lot of stress off her, and I wanted to help get things as efficient and organized as possible so she could breathe a bit easier by the time I went back work. Time itself, it turned out, was a very precious thing.

As I mentioned earlier, when Collin was sleeping, it was the time to get stuff done around the house but without waking him up—a tricky balance. When I was in the military, I was very tactical while on a patrol or waiting in an ambush; it was an art I think I'd mastered pretty well. But "new dad, baby quiet" tactician required a master class in sneaking around. It reminds me of a horror movie when the soon-to-be victim is hiding somewhere with their hands over their mouths and the tension just feels amplified. When Collin was sleeping, it was like every squeaky floor board in the house was under my every step. I could hear my own heartbeat.

Cell phones were the worst, and I was terrible with mine. I am not the type of person with my head glued to a screen 24/7, but I'm a huge fan of my iPhone and could set a different tone for email, text, Facebook messages, and so on. But even with the volume down low, it was the loudest sound in the world with a sleeping newborn. There were countless times when Kelly kicked me under the covers because my phone was making a sound. After I was blown up overseas, I pretty much lost the hearing in my right ear and now I wear a hearing aid. But at night when I take it off and I'm lying on my right side and my good ear, I am more or less deaf. I can hear loud sounds like Collin crying, the dogs barking, my alarm clock, or the fire alarm, but ring tones on a low setting? Not so much. I'm grateful to be alive, though, as I'm sure Kelly wanted to kill me on multiple occasions because of those damn ringtones.

Another thing I had to learn was "Collin Time." No matter how much you plan or schedule, Collin or his travel bag would usually have the last word. It was easier to hit a target on time in the military than get anywhere on time with Collin. Packing his diaper bag, for example, was like preparing for a mission; everything has to be easy to reach and organized just so. There are diapers, wipes, chew toys, regular toys, extra shirts, pants, socks, diaper rash cream, stuff for teething. There is also stuff stashed under his stroller and in every pocket in the car. Kelly makes it look easy and for the most part, as long as I pack the diaper bag, it's easy for me to find what we need. But when I get home from being at work, the training starts anew.

When Collin gets fussy, the teething ring comes out from Pocket A. He spits up, grab the extra bib from Pocket B next to the diapers. When he's hungry, a bottle is prepped and ready to go in Pocket C with an extra bib and shirt in case it spills. This is a straight-up, full-on tactical operation, and Kelly is a "Tier 1" operator when it comes to it. As for me, I'm more like a Marine eating a crayon, but new dads have to start somewhere.

As Collin got older, we would take him out to a few places such as the grocery store and pharmacy and grandma's house. As it got warmer, Kelly took him to Walmart. What I find interesting is that Collin loves Walmart and will stay content in his carrier without an issue, but when Kelly takes him to Michaels for decoratives or supplies, he has a meltdown within five minutes. Kelly would have to leave the store because he was making such a scene. It's a mystery. But he's getting better and did very well when we took him to Panera and Jamba Juice.

At the end of the day, life with a newborn will be as good as your routines. But I also learned pretty quickly that even having a solid, well-thought-out routine is no match for the unpredictability of a baby. I mean, how many times a day can something so small poop?!

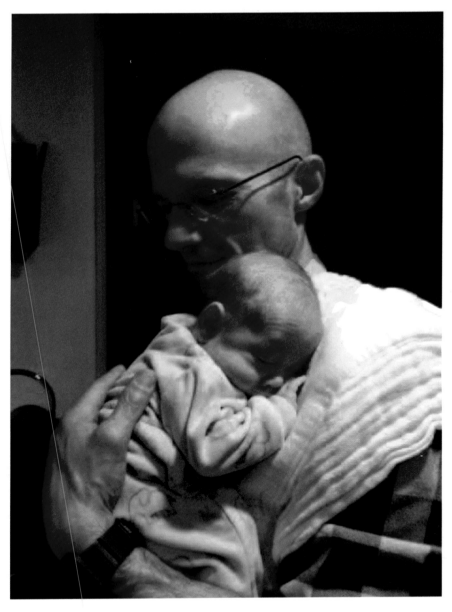

Me holding Collin on my last night before I headed back to Kabul, Afghanistan on Feb 6, 2019.

The famous Crossed Swords in Baghdad, Iraq taken sometime in Nov 2005 while working with Blackwater.

This picture was taken Regional Embassy Office (RIO) in Erbil, Iraq in May 2005, while working with Blackwater.

Blackwater Aviation door gunner, taken in Oct 2009, while on contract with Blackwater USA.

2019 Boston Savage Race, first race of the season after Collin being born.

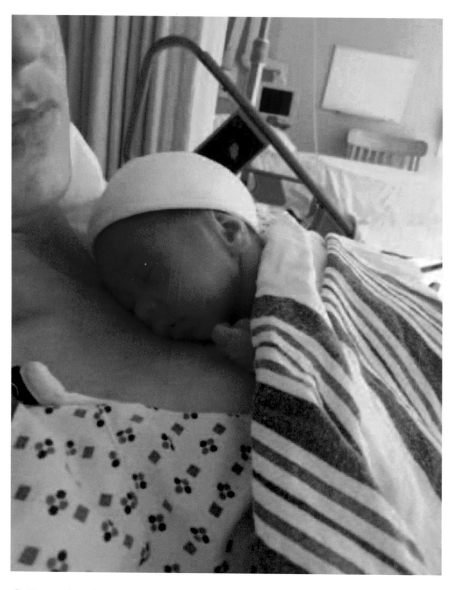

Collin right after he was born before they rushed him off to the NICU.
3 lbs 14 oz.

Me fast asleep after feeding Collin. I was so tired if I sat still for more than 2 minutes I would fall asleep.

Kelly holding Collin after his bottle. He loves his mama.

Collin sitting up on his own. This picture was taken by Kelly in June 2019 just prior to me coming home from Kabul for leave.

Collin loves this swing and would spend hours in it. It was great for getting him to take naps. Taken in July 2019.

CHAPTER 12

Just Like That, Back to Work

···

AS LONG AS I have worked overseas, it seems my time at home always goes by way too fast, and this time was no exception. I was home from December 12 to February 6, and with being so busy with Collin, those eight weeks flew by in a flash. In the past when I was single, I would look forward to going back because I was always fortunate to be on great teams with some solid shooters. Work for me was like being with family except in a combat zone. Guys in my line of work called each other "Brother" and we meant it. I've worked with some of the same guys for more than fifteen years, and to this day I still trust them with my life. We joke and bust each other's balls relentlessly, but that's only because of the bond we have. We talk shit with each other as a sign of respect and no one ever worries. You worry when they don't talk shit about you because that means you aren't liked or respected.

But as I started dating Kelly, going back to work became harder and harder. And now with Collin, this was by far the hardest trip back to work I've ever had. I not only miss out on all the little stuff, but in a way I feel like I'm abandoning my family, and it sucks. Kelly and I have often talked about this and in the end, because I make a good living, we both agreed that the sacrifice we make now will make our future more stable and provide a better life for our children. It gives us the ability to invest into retirement and, pending any major life catastrophe, I expect to retire by the time I'm fifty-five. This may sound nice, but that brings me to another topic: What will I do with myself? I guess it's a good thing I own a farm.

So all I can do is go back to work and stick to my routine. But there's something else that bothers me. After spending the last eight weeks with Collin and watching how fast he was growing, I was nervous not just because I was leaving Kelly alone to take care of him, but I was worried about him forgetting me. I knew from talking with Kelly that when I did come back, there would be an adjustment and she told me to expect it. But knowing that didn't help much, and definitely kept me up at night.

Over the last several years, I have always stuck to a 90/30-day rotation between work and home. In the past when I was single, I might stay deployed up to ten months, come home for a week or two, then go back over, but things are different now. With Collin being born early and shifting my family leave earlier, I'd be in Kabul from February 8 to June 16—a little over four months. So it was really tough to leave.

Kelly and Collin were both asleep when I got up at 2 a.m. to get ready for my 3:30 pickup. I gave myself twenty minutes to go back to bed just to see them. In my line of work, you learn how to separate home from your job, so I kissed Collin and Kelly on the forehead and caught my ride to the airport without looking back. I always respected the guys I worked with who had families back home, but until you have one of your own, you never truly understand what they are going through.

Going back on the road was the first time I realized how really tired I was. I got to the airport, boarded the early morning flight from Hartford to Washington Dulles, and passed out immediately until the plane landed in DC. I went through my routine at Dulles, grabbing some breakfast and a couple of drinks for the flight, and once onboard, I passed out again and slept for the first eight hours of the flight, the longest stretch of sleep I'd had in over six weeks.

Getting through the Dubai airport is relatively simple for the size of it, but due to the number of international travelers who use it, you run into all sorts of characters, from Chinese tourists taking pictures to drunk Russians to your typically rude Europeans. I know American travelers have a "reputation," but I can tell you from experience that they are the easiest, most organized, and detailed-oriented when traveling overseas—much better behaved than when they travel in the US.

I checked into my favorite hotel, the Hilton Dubai Creek, got some lunch and sat by the pool, then planned to visit the Mall of Dubai. I had an hour to kill, so I lay down in my bed, and the next thing I knew it was 10 p.m. I had slept for another eight hours. It's crazy how your body recovers, so I just took a shower and went right back to sleep until my early morning flight to Kabul.

When I fly into Kabul, I take Emirates Airlines, and it's like stepping back in time. Now I'm the first to talk trash about European travelers, but the Afghanis are simply out of control. For example, they have no concept of lines and will rush the check-in counter. Fortunately, Emirate flight attendants are pretty tough and put them right in their place. It's kind of funny, because most

Muslim men don't take it lightly when a woman yells at them. But here they are, intimidated by these flight attendants—they just don't take any shit.

Working for the State Department has some benefits when it comes to clearing customs. For example, we have our own transportation on and off the plane so we go in a separate direction than the locals, which is a good thing because you can bet that more than a handful are Taliban and might be looking for an opportunity to attack an infidel. Fortunately, that has yet to happen at this airport due to the security and some competent Afghanis. You can also thank US taxpayer dollars, but that's a story for another time.

Once I clear customs and make it back to our airbase, I hop on a chopper once again for the short flight to the embassy and, BAM! I'm right back at it. Whenever I get back to my room in Kabul, I sometimes feel guilty because I've been here so long it really does feel like a home away from home. Since I'm a senior Foreign Service officer, I qualify for either a studio apartment or a full-size one bedroom, and I choose the studio. I don't spend much time in the room anyway, and when I look back on all the crap I've collected over the last five years, I can only wonder how much more I'd be stuffing in a one bedroom.

My main goal when I walk in the door is to get to unpack my bag, grab some chow, and call home to let Kelly know I made it back safe and sound. Once all that is done, I jump into bed so I can get up early and start my routine, which is the key to survival here in Kabul, especially my next rotation home would not be until June 15—seventeen weeks away!

Still, I always enjoy my first day back from R&R because it's an admin day. I can pretty much do what I want. So I check my email, confirm my schedule, and check in with the staff. This time I was really excited to see everyone so I could report on how well Collin was doing since I left rather quickly on emergency leave back in December. These first twenty-four hours also give me a chance to get acclimated because for anyone who has been overseas, it's super noisy, and it takes a while to get used to hearing the normal daily sounds of generators and helicopters.

For some reason, on this trip back I had trouble sleeping the first couple of nights. It was probably because I really missed my family and still felt terrible about leaving Kelly all alone back at home to take care of everything: Collin, Brett, the dogs, the house, even Sniffles the cat (though I preferred to call her Snickers). It's a good thing that Kelly's family lives so close since Cindy comes over a lot and is a huge help. Still, I'm not sure how Kelly pulls it off. Every improvement Collin made was because of her; I won't take credit for any of it. I may work overseas in some of the most hostile environments in the world, but it's nothing compared to what she goes through as a mother. I know how hard it can be even if she doesn't show it. And I know I keep saying it, but she's an amazing woman, and I'm very lucky to have her as a wife.

Once back in the office I'd be covering the morning shift, which went from 6 a.m. to 6 p.m. six days a week with a shorter day on Friday. This wasn't too bad as every other week or so I would end up with a day off to make the time go by faster. I was also wrapping up my last three classes for my second bachelor's degree so I'd be keeping pretty busy this rotation. And since my next R&R in June lined up with a couple of Tough Mudders and the Savage Race in Boston, I'd be super committed to my training. I'd also signed up to compete in the 44 – 46 Masters group at the 2019 CrossFit Open. I had all the motivation I needed!

As time went on and I rolled through the first couple of weeks back in Kabul, my routine fell into a new norm. I would get up at 2 a.m. to work out, come back to my room to shower and eat breakfast, call home to say goodnight, and then go to work. Once I was done with my shift, I'd go back to my room do some homework and be in bed by 7:30 or 8. Then I'd get up and do it all over again. Now many of you may wonder about that six hours of sleep per night, which I agree is not a lot. But after being home with Collin for the last eight weeks where six hours of solid sleep never happened, I was making out like a bandit!

Once back at work, I was able to talk to Kelly daily via Skype and see both her and Collin. For the most part, she was doing great, but I could easily tell she was tired. It was very important to never say anything about getting sleep now that I was back at work. Collin continued with his weekly doctors' appointments and Kelly's hard work and feedings every two hours kept putting weight on him. He was still having issues with spitting up and getting bad diaper rashes, though, so they put him on a liquid form of Nexium because they believed he had acid reflux. But because he was still under six months old, it was hard to give him certain medications until he put on more weight. Kelly was hardly producing milk anymore so we decided that she stop pumping and switch Collin to formula for every meal. The search for the perfect formula also continued.

I'd only been gone a few weeks but each time I talked to Kelly and saw Collin, I was convinced he was growing. Kelly told me I was crazy, but for anyone who has ever deployed overseas in the military or worked far away from home, life goes on back in the States, and it's important to stay connected with that any way you can. For me a lot of that was through Collin.

My days in Kabul soon became weeks and I continued to march forward like any good solider. Getting up at 2 a.m. wasn't always easy. It meant the CrossFit gym would be relatively clear since it was usually packed by the time I got off work at 6 p.m., but it's outside and February in Kabul is cold. Still, I consider my morning gym routine like ripping off a Band-Aid. My alarm goes off, I slam a pre-workout drink, throw on some clothes, and am out the door in less than five minutes. Average temperature: about 19 to 20 degrees Fahrenheit, which makes the metal weight-lifting bars pretty frigid. After about thirty minutes, the cold seeps up into my forearms and things get harder to lift. But as busy as the embassy is, it's nice to have a workout area to yourself no matter how cold. And by the time the 6 a.m. class shows up, I'm gone.

After the gym I'm usually lucky enough to get in a quick goodnight call back home, but between 7:30 and 8 is what we came to describe as Collin's "bewitching hour" which can be forty-five minutes of pure hell for Kelly. It was the same block of time he was most active during Kelly's entire pregnancy. Kelly swore he was doing cartwheels because the kid was all over the place. Even to this day he tends to be a restless sleeper, and I have no idea where he gets that from. I also liked calling home at night because I was always able to talk to Brett, who in the morning would normally have already left for the bus.

After calling home I would jump in the shower and get dressed, leaving me twenty to thirty minutes before I had to leave for work—a five-minute walk so I could take me time. Then all I had to do when I got to the office was pull up my chair and get a turnover from the night-shift guy. That gave me plenty of time to get my notes together for our 7:30 mission brief, grab some break-fast, and get my computer up and running.

I know that I've mentioned many times how I love my job and I do, but the reason I love it and why I'm so good at it is because of the guys who work for me. They make me look like a rock star, and to take any credit for that would be a shame. I have the responsibility of owning everything they do, and when I make a command decision, whether it involves a "kinetic event" (such as a terrorist attack or a natural disaster) or routine protective operations, it's all on me. Any wrong decision could cause people to lose their lives and put my ass in front of Congress. I don't ever want to be in that position, and my great team members have helped to keep it that way.

CHAPTER 13

More Midwife Drama

·······································

AS COLLIN CONTINUED to make remarkable gains in his weight, Kelly's postpartum routines pretty much fell into place—until the midwife showed up again. As you may recall, Kelly had continued with both the midwife and OBGYN appointments until December 7 when Collin was born. I figured at that point it was safe to say there would be no more midwife, or so I thought. About a week or two after Kelly reached out to Janet to ask her about billing and a refund since Collin wasn't born at the house, Janet declared that there was no refund, and we still owed her a balance of $2,000.

Kelly and I were confused. Why was there a balance for services she never provided? Janet explained that she still planned to be responsible for postcare with Kelly once the baby came home. I don't remember ever hearing that part of the deal. To make matters worse, Kelly told me she wasn't happy with Janet because of an incident with her at the hospital when she came up to visit after Collin was born. What did I miss during my flight home from Kabul?!

Kelly explained that the day after Collin was born, Janet stopped by the hospital to see how they were doing. My mother-in-law and brother-in-law were there, and when Janet came into the room, she smelled like marijuana. When my wife asked her about it, she replied that it must have been from a bud or something she had in her pocket. And since the marijuana was prescribed to her by a doctor, it was no big deal anyway. But to my wife it was definitely a big deal and as she described the scene, I also became concerned.

My issue is that whether or not the marijuana was prescribed, it's a drug that alters one's mental state, no different than drinking or taking certain prescription medications. So what was it doing in the room of a newborn preemie? Would she have been that way if she had actually delivered our baby at home—or any baby, for that matter? If I drank a beer or took a pain pill and then attempted to do my job, it would be illegal. You would think the same would apply to a midwife, or am I missing something here? My wife showed me all the text messages and emails between her and Janet. She wasn't taking no for an answer and told Kelly she would take legal action if we didn't pay her the balance. Kelly and I looked at each other and said, *The hell with that. We'll see her in court if it comes to it.*

In the second week of January, we received a certified letter from Janet demanding the remaining balance of $2,100. If she didn't get it by February 22, failure to pay would lead to legal action. We decided to seek legal advice because in the end we would rather pay a lawyer $2,100 than this crazy broad. Now one would think that finding a lawyer would be simple, but in Connecticut this is considered "small claims" and most lawyers aren't interested. We finally found a great lawyer, and even though he decided not to take the case, he gave us free legal advice which was really cool of him.

When we met the lawyer, he looked over our agreement and said that since it wasn't an actual contract, we could take the midwife to court for a partial refund of our original payment. But we didn't want any of our money back; we just wanted this wacky chick out of our lives. He further advised us that if it did go to court, the judge could decide either way. In short, we had a 50/50 chance of losing or winning the case. He suggested that we write her a letter stating that we won't pay her the requested amount because her services weren't needed since Collin had an emergency delivery, but to keep the $2,500 we'd already paid as a good-faith gesture.

So Kelly and I drafted a courteous and professional letter explaining all of this to Janet, sent it to her via registered mail, and hoped for the best. Since I'd soon be heading back to work, we decided there was nothing more to do than wait for her answer. Once back at work, I'd ask Kelly if she'd heard anything and six weeks later we finally did.

Around mid-March Kelly received a letter from Janet's attorney announcing that she'd be suing us for $4,000, so we decided to get our own lawyer. Since I was back in Afghanistan and Kelly was the only one mentioned in the lawsuit, there wasn't much I could do. Kelly went back to the attorney who helped us for some more advice and he once again declined to take the case because it would be in small claims court. He still helped us out, and we decided to roll the dice.

At the end of April Kelly got the letter requesting her appearance in court in June, which was good because I'd be home by then and we would have several weeks to get ready. Kelly became a legal expert on midwife cases like ours while I did my own research. After all that, we decided our chances were still

50/50. I was hoping not to pay *anything*, but after talking with Kelly, we both agreed that if we only had to pay the remaining balance, we'd take it. I recall the final amount she was suing us for was $4,747 which included attorney and court fees. Game on.

One of the main issues we were having is that Connecticut does not require a license to practice independent midwifery—there are license requirements for Nurse Midwifes only. So filing a complaint with the state did no good because Janet didn't need a license. Who knew? But I still feel like a dumbass.

What I also discovered is that while home births are legal in Connecticut, they can only take place in the presence of a licensed nurse midwife. For Janet to have performed a home birth legally, she needed that supervision, and I don't recall ever hearing about that. I began to wonder if she'd been doing this without one and for how long and if there had been any issues or lawsuits.

As I think back to all the times we met with Janet, there were several trip wires I should have caught. But Janet was so nonchalant about everything, I never made those connections. One of them was the fact that she wanted to be paid in cash, and then she would charge the health insurance company $7,000. So even though you wouldn't be able to itemize the full amount on your taxes, you would get most of it back once you met the deductible. I did flag this right away, but like most folks I didn't mind shorting the IRS if I could, so count me in.

The second missed flag is that whenever she gave medical advice, she always insisted that in the end it was your choice. I think this is how she covered her ass if anything went wrong, something she could use if she needed to. Initially she didn't even want Kelly to see her OBGYN doctor for checkups, but I'm sure glad we did. Only as long as the doc kept giving us a green light would we go forward with the home birth. And look what happened: red light, emergency C-section!

I felt helpless being in Kabul while Kelly was going through all this and still being on point with Collin. It was taking a toll on her, so I decided to reach out to my cousin Brian who's a lawyer and ask for some help. We've always been close, so he was happy to pitch in. He talked to Kelly a few times, and she sent him copies of all the paperwork, including the court documents and the complaint form we wanted to send to the Connecticut Department of Health. Even though Connecticut doesn't license independent midwives, getting something on file would, at a minimum, create a paper trail, so that if she ever did anything like this again, we hoped it would set off an alarm (though I doubted it).

Now every difficult thing is a learning experience, right? As long as you can take something useful away from it, then all is not lost. So when we decided to ask my cousin to get involved, I was about to learn one of those lessons: never mix business with family. When we first asked him for help, he came out of the gate running and then suddenly stopped replying to our texts and emails. He didn't even return a phone message. I didn't expect him to do this for free and told him to bill me like a regular client—which he agreed to do—but when I say nothing, I mean nothing. I never heard from him again.

At this point there was nothing further either Kelly or I could do other than come up with a plan in case my cousin was a no-show and then wait until I got back home, which was still about eight weeks away. So I decided to research how small claims court works in Connecticut so we could be prepared.

Small claims court seemed pretty simple: You can only file lawsuits for monetary damages and for no more than $5,000. Most small claims disputes tend to be landlord-tenant matters. Court fees run about $90 to $100, so if we lost, the court fee would be minimal. Legal representation isn't required and both plaintiffs and defendants can represent themselves. Janet had an attorney, but since the dispute was going to small claims, her lawyer also declined to represent her. We still wanted a lawyer because there was still a chance this could all be taken care of without even going to court.

During the entire process, Kelly and I wondered about issuing a counter-claim, but we decided to let Janet keep what was paid in good faith because prior to this whole thing smelling like a hospital bed pan and it being a little weird anyway, Kelly had no issues with Janet, and we also figured it would look good in court to not be asking for money back. Who would have known that this would not be the best decision? We could have also requested that the case be transferred to the regular or superior court. With 20/20 hindsight this may have been a better idea since Janet was not in the position to take it that far. As I always told Kelly, I would rather pay a lawyer several thousand dollars than give Janet a penny, just out of spite.

For the most part we stuck to our plan and printed out all the correspondence Kelly had with Janet and all cash payment receipts since the lawsuit was against Kelly. I would be a witness in case one was needed. With all of our ducks lined up, there was nothing left to do except decide what to wear, where to park, how to address the judge. and other common-sense stuff that most adults can figure out. But even re-reading what I just wrote made me wonder the kinds of people who show up to court without a basic understanding on how to present themselves. I would often joke with Kelly that I didn't care if we won or lost, as long as it didn't turn out to be like an episode of *Judge Judy*.

As I was reading up about what to do and not do at small claims court, I learned that the one thing they stress is to try to work things out on your own prior to coming to court. I didn't tell Kelly this, but I did make one final attempt to ask Janet if we could be adults about this and come to an agreement. I even did the math on how many weeks Kelly was pregnant before we contacted Janet and agreed to pay an additional $500 and call it a day at $3,000. But she refused, telling me that I was insulting her profession and the only way an agreement could be reached was if I paid her the complete balance. I wrote her one final letter declining her "offer" and countered that if she agreed to the final $500 payment, I wouldn't file a complaint with the Connecticut Department of Health. Her final correspondence told me to stop threatening her and she would see us in court. So be it. I filed the complaint and let the legal system take care of the rest.

I still had eight weeks at the embassy before going home and decided to concentrate on wrapping up the CrossFit Open and my bachelor's degree and making sure that everything at home was good to go for Kelly, Collin, and Brett. It was mid-March—still winter in Connecticut—and we were still getting snow with everyone getting antsy waiting for the final thaw. Since our house was more than 200 years old, we were on the verge of needing a new septic tank, which was no longer draining into the leach field because the field was saturated with rain from the fall and all the melting snow.

Collin was still doing great and putting on weight. Brett was doing well in school. The two dogs were happy enough. Kelly was holding down the fort, which made it easier for me to concentrate on life here in Kabul. The only thing to really do was count down the days until I went home in June and hope the septic tank held out until the summer.

CHAPTER 14

Growing Like a Weed

·····································

WHEN THEY SAY babies grow fast, they aren't lying. My little poop machine was growing like a weed. Maybe it's because I see him every day when I talk to Kelly on Skype. During my career overseas, I noticed this a lot with my friends' kids but even more so with my nieces and nephews. Even Brett grew up fast as he had just turned six when I first met him and now as I write this is getting ready to be a freshman in high school.

It's hard to believe Collin's size these days when I remember he was less than four pounds when he was born. After we got him home he averaged gaining about a pound a week and slowly hitting all the goals set by his pediatrician. It's hard to believe that at one point the doctor was thinking of readmitting him to the NICU again if he didn't break ten pounds by a certain time. No problem there.

Kelly's mother bought us a baby scale and we were able to weigh him daily. At about nine pounds Kelly could feed him at 8 p.m. and let him go three-to-four hours between eating until breakfast. This meant he could rest a little more, which also helped him grow. Finally, we were able to introduce other soft foods into his diet. Because Collin never really picked up on the whole concept of breast feeding, baby formula was his main staple for calories, but we had lots of flexibility for introducing new foods to him. We also had to use common sense. When we did introduce something new into his diet, we would wait every two days or so to see if he had any type of allergic reaction.

The first "real food" Kelly gave Collin was a banana because they were the easiest to mash up and the kid loves them. She also tried peaches, plums, blueberries, and strawberries which he loves as well. Tomatoes were next and that led to avocado. Still no allergic reactions, so next time we went to the doctor I asked about adding peanut butter to the list. It's not only my favorite snack in the world, but if he was going to have a bad reaction to food, it was more than likely going to be peanut butter. At first, we tried powdered peanut butter mixed with water which he liked, but wasn't crazy about. Then we decided to mix it with formula, but he would spit it out. When Kelly gave him actual peanut butter, he ate it up without a problem! As his food palette became more refined, we continued—with his doctor's approval—to introduce different types of food. He was still working on his chewing skills, but we tried scrambled eggs and rice, which he seemed to like but had a hard time processing. I mean, the kid didn't have teeth yet.

Now that Collin was born, Kelly wanted to go back to being a vegetarian and had this idea that Collin would be one as well, but that wasn't going to happen on my watch. I don't have anything against vegetarians, but it's never been part of my lifestyle. Kelly's not a true vegetarian, because she still eats seafood. And she doesn't mind cooking meat for Brett and I. So after discussing the issue at length with Collin's pediatrician, he advised that as long as we kept certain proteins in his diet, there was nothing wrong with having your infant eat as a vegetarian.

Here is the thing, though: I'm Italian and grew up eating traditional meals with my family which often included meatballs, sausage, pork, or veal. So Kelly and I agreed that Collin could eat meat when I'm home or when he's at his grandmother's or uncle's house and that with Kelly he would stick to eating mostly vegetarian meals. But then the doctor told us it was important that Collin eat all the different meat proteins to help with nutrition and his developmental process. If later he wanted to become a vegetarian, he could make his own choice. Italians – 1, Vegetarians – 0.

As I've said, the biggest change I noticed in Collin was how fast he was physically growing, Kelly went through two different diaper sizes in under four months, which was crazy compared to where we were back in December. He was so small when he was born that the smallest diaper for premature babies were still too big for him. At five weeks Collin was still developing fat in his body, and every time I changed his diaper, I swear he had the saggy ass of a ninety-year-old man. It's kind of the circle of life, right? We start wearing diapers after entering this world and many of us will do so while leaving it.

Collin was also outgrowing everything else he wore, from socks to shirts and even bibs. Kelly could barely keep up with him. He was growing so fast that he'd wear certain outfits only a couple of times before we had donate them. Fortunately, friends and family brought us enough clothes to last for months.

What I found especially amazing was his overall developmental skills. Even though he was still small by typical standards, his cognitive skills were improving right on track with the norm, going from a regular rattle to basic toys to toys with more sounds, shapes, and sizes. My mother-in-law was always bringing him something to play with, and there were two toys in particular that Collin seemed to really gravitate toward. One was a gel-type play pad that was filled with fish and aquatic characters; the other was this piano-type play pad he could lay on and kick the bejesus out of with his feet.

The second one was especially cool because it had sit, kneel, and stand-up settings that would last him another year or two. It also had a mobile setup with different safari animals of a dozen different colors that made multiple noises. Heck, I wanted to play with it! It was such a wonder to watch how the human mind develops as infants experience things for the very first time. It gave me a new appreciation for the true innocence of a child before they are exposed to all the horrors of the world. It also makes protecting one's children take on a whole other perspective, one you never really understand until you have a child of your own. I would give my life for Collin and not think twice about it.

Sleeping arrangements for Collin were drastically changing along with everything else. During the first couple of months, Kelly used what they call a Moses Basket for Collin to sleep in, and since he was under twenty pounds, it was also easier to carry him around the house in it. It made the little dude a lot more mobile. At ninety days, he finally outgrew it, and this where some controversy came in.

Both my mother-in-law and my mother got together and had a "day bed" made for Collin. I called it an eyesore and it sure wasn't cheap. The concept was pretty good—it was shaped like a quarter moon and it even lit up. But I didn't really know what it was for because it wasn't a bassinet and definitely wasn't a crib.

Due to its size we had to put it in the formal living room, but that didn't turn out to be practical, and in the end, Collin did not use it much and outgrew it in just a few months. Then it was off to the barn with everything else he stopped using to donate or put on eBay. So check your listings because this thing is "on the market." I'm sure that by the time you read this it will hopefully be gone. If not, I will change the listing to free, but you'll have to pick it up. Wait! I may do local delivery if I'm home.

Putting the whole moon bed thing aside, the next thing Collin outgrew was the bassinet we kept in our bedroom. When I was overseas, he'd stay there during the day and sleep in bed with Kelly at night. Yeah, yeah, we know you shouldn't do that. But sometimes you do what you gotta do to keep balance in the universe.

When I got home, Brett and I moved Collin's crib from this very small room into our bedroom and started to prepare the bigger second-guest bedroom for him. This way as Collin got older, he'd would already have more space, and between you and me, that little room he was in always creeped me out a bit. If any room in this big house is haunted, it's probably that one. Much better to be safe than sorry when it comes to the little guy. Moving the crib into our bedroom was also a good move because he's used to sleeping in it, and when we move it to the bigger room, it will be an easier adjustment for him. If all goes well, that would happen in October or November right before he turns one, which would keep us in line with his normal developmental steps.

One concern we had as Collin got older was that he seemed a little behind when it came to rolling over. I mean, the kid hated it. He felt more comfortable on his back and hated tummy time. Once again it was Kelly to the rescue, and once he finally got used to rolling over, he became a lot more mobile. When he started sitting up on his own, it was game on, and before we knew it, he was on his hands and knees. He wasn't quite crawling yet but rocking back and forth, which lead to this inch worm thing he did with his head. It was funny to watch, but it showed how adaptive kids can be.

I also noticed how adaptive he was when it came to communication. Up until now he would cry when he was hungry, needed to be changed, was bored, or got cold, but as he got older, he re-learned different sounds. Crying was still a primary strategy because he knew it got an immediate response from his mother, but certain sounds such as coughing started to mean certain things. I never really got the meaning of them because I was gone so much, but Kelly learned to read him very well, and I was amazed at how well she was able to communicate with him.

Overall, he was a happy baby and always had a smile on his face, but you could tell when he got frustrated, and it would happen in a flash. One second he's laughing, and then BAM! the grin goes away, and he starts flailing his hands and screaming; I find it funny when I see it, but Kelly tells me to not let Collin see me laugh or he'll think that type of behavior is acceptable. Everyone says he gets that from me, and as I spent more and more time with him, I realized, holy shit, they are spot on! I'm usually smiling and generally in a good mood but can change in a split second. So I tell everyone he has his mother's personality and his father's temper. He'll be a kind, friendly, and caring person like Brett but won't let anyone push him around. That quality has helped me in many stressful situations including during combat. Let's face it: the world can be both a very beautiful and very scary place. Having the ability to turn your emotions on and off—and knowing when to do that—can come in handy.

Collin is still a little behind the power curve when it comes to normal height and weight for his age, but he's making great strides. By the time he turns one, he will have probably caught up. But since both Kelly and I are both on the smaller side, he may end up that way as well. Right now we're focusing on his mental ability and development and, according to all the doctors, it's right where it needs to be. And if you look at how Kelly and I turned out, there's nothing wrong with being a little guy. Especially if he's anything like me because I am a frickin' pit bull.

Speaking of pit bulls, Collin began to show an interest in our dogs and for the most part all has been going well. Clarice the pit bull, who we adopted, is a big puppy and loves everyone. Winnie the bulldog is still a puppy and a bit of a wild card but great with Collin, always wanting to jump up and lick his face. We keep both dogs out of our formal living room because of how much they shed, so the interaction between them and Collin has been limited. We know that will change once he becomes mobile, and we are almost there.

All in all, Collin has made leaps and bounds in the few months since being born and to see his transformation is truly amazing. I remember holding him and thinking how small he was and couldn't imagine him outgrowing his preemie diapers and especially his Moses basket and now sleeping in his crib. Now the kid's about to turn one and to say that time is flying by is an understatement. Being away from home is becoming harder and harder.

CHAPTER 15

Staying in Contact

···

COMPARED TO how it was growing up and especially from when I first joined the military back in the 1990s, I can't imagine how hard it must have been for parents to be away from their families for long periods of time. Being single made it no big deal for me, and for years I would just call my parents and grandmother each week. I never realized what some of my friends were likely going through being away from their wife (or husband) and children.

Today's new smartphone technology has totally changed all that—instant communication anywhere in the world at my fingertips. On my cell phone I have instant messaging, FaceTime, Facebook, Skype, and there are others. Staying in contact with my family is as easy as it can be. As long as I can re-member, I have always considered myself pretty reliable at keeping in touch with friends and family. But as time goes on with work and now family, it's getting more and more difficult, and I can't imagine how it would have been, say, twenty years ago. At least now I can just shoot out a text or an instant message to say hello. I can't believe I'm saying this, but "kids these days" will never know what it was like "back then" and take for granted these amazing technological advancements.

My current rotation is a little over four months, and as busy as Kelly is, she's great with keeping me in the loop with everything going on. Since Collin is pretty much on a schedule, daily phone calls are relatively easy, especially since I'm working nights. Kelly sends me multiple pictures every day of Collin doing one thing or another, and it's almost like watching a constant movie of his life, and he's changing. To me it was crazy how fast time was going by, but if you ask Kelly, maybe not so much since she's the one feeding Collin every couple of hours.

Skype is our go-to when it comes to back-and-forth communication, but Facebook and FaceTime, to name a few, have their place. But since Kelly is not a big fan of technology, we usually stick with Skype because it's the easiest to use, but even that can be hit or miss depending on the internet connection. Even when it's bad, Skype tends to be the most reliable, and worst-case scenario I can always make a phone call. I prefer FaceTime to Skype since it automatically links all the message contacts from my phone, giving me a direct link to everyone. But since my wife is not quite in sync with modern technology, we use Skype. And as long as that makes Mama happy, I'm good to go with it.

We mostly communicate via texting because it's easier, and I always have my phone on me, especially when overseas. Sprint is our provider, and I've used them for almost twenty years, even when other providers came out with better deals. If there's any kind of problem, it's usually resolved with a quick phone call to customer service. Why bother changing?

The only time that communicating is hard is when I am actually at work, because in a classified space, no electronic devices are allowed. In that case I use email and Kelly does the same, especially if any sort of emergency happens. I just have to make sure I keep her in the loop when it comes to my schedule. Worst case she can call my desk and someone will pick up the line 24/7. When calling work from home, even though the call is international, it gets routed through a DC switchboard, so it's just like calling any out-of-state phone number.

With all these ways to communicate, I still look forward to getting cards and packages. Kelly can really think outside of the box, and whenever she sends me stuff, it always has things I really need and some of the most random things you could think of. I especially appreciate it when she sends me food because while she knows I like to eat healthy, she insists I'm too skinny, so she sends me a lot of stuff I end up giving away, but I do try most of it. What drives her crazy is when I measure my food out to monitor my caloric daily intake. I do this not to lose weight but to make sure I'm eating enough when I'm training for a race. By keeping track of my "healthy" calories, I keep from going under my set daily amount. So what does she do? Sends me boxes of cereal and candy and crosses out all the nutritional information with a Sharpie with notes on the packaging that tell me to shut up and eat it. I think it's funny and cool that she does all this, but with Collin taking up a majority of her time, I don't get as many packages. But when I do, she still goes all out.

And to emphasize how really cool she is, I was competing in a race back in 2017 and asked her to send me nude pictures as a pre-race motivator. When I arrived at the hotel and started to unpack, there was an envelope in my bag marked "Nude Pic from Mama." Now I'd be lying if I said I didn't get all excited, but when I opened the envelope there weren't any pictures, just a stick figure drawing of a nude women that reminded me of something a kid would do. To this very day I still laugh over this and am snickering right now as I write all this down!

Skyping daily with both Kelly and Collin is a huge morale boost when overseas, and I also like being able to chat with everyone directly. Since we have the option of using either our phones or computer, I tend to Skype directly from my computer when in my room and phone when outside my room with the exception of work. At home Kelly needs to be more mobile and uses her phone so she can move around with it. It has a protective case since Collin is too young to understand how a phone works, but he can hold it and throw it. One thing we both learned is that he can make the phone do stuff you might not want it to do such as lock a screen or set some mode that you can never get out of and you end of spending an hour on YouTube watching videos that explain how to undo whatever it was he did. And it's not just your phone; the kid will change settings on your FitBit or iWatch if you don't pay attention. They are all toys to him.

Back in the day, I would call home every week, usually on Sunday, but once I was in the military and after 9/11, my weekly calls were subject to OPSEC protocols (operational security). This weekly phone call was pivotal for my family, and even if I missed a call, no news was generally good news. With the exception of a few friends, no one really asked questions about what I was doing overseas—which was a good thing, especially for my mother and grandmother—and they always respected good OPSEC.

My wife is amazing when it comes to OPSEC, since being married to me doesn't mean I tell her everything. She rarely asks questions and when she does will always check to see if it's something I can talk about. I do keep her informed as much as I can, but let me get this straight: my work is not exactly supersecret but in the end, the less one talks about it the better. If something did happen when I was in Pakistan and especially now in Kabul, my wife will ask if it impacted me and I can give a simple Yes or No answer. If something scary does happen, I send a quick text out to everyone saying that I'm fine and not affected by what they might have seen on the news. Best to keep it all simple.

With modern technology comes modern-day issues and when overseas, communications can be spotty depending upon where you are. The internet we have in Kabul is decent enough depending on the time of day you use it. I noticed when I was working days, for example, that I never had a problem talking with Kelly when I got up at 4 a.m. when most of the embassy is asleep.

In those rare cases when the internet is down, I can still pick up the phone and dial out like I was back in the States since our switchboard is wired that way. It also means that in case of an emergency, someone can call me directly as well. I also have a local cell phone which I pay for myself. I keep my phone card charged so that even if the shit hits the fan, I can make calls or at least send a text to everyone letting them know I'm okay. I also have my regular cell phone with Sprint that I've used for the last nineteen years. Their international rates aren't the best, but texting is free and if I have to make an emergency call, I couldn't care less what it cost.

Over the first few months of being away after Collin was born, seeing him daily by Skype is pretty cool. Not only do I get to talk to Kelly and Brett, but I interact with Collin as well. I really enjoyed Skyping when Kelly was feeding him because that's when he seemed the happiest. I mean, who doesn't like to eat, so why wouldn't he be happy? My biggest fear, as I've said before, is that he will not only forget about me but, even more importantly, be scared of me when I come home. I know that being on a computer screen is nowhere near the same as being in front of him in person, but at least he can hear my voice.

Collin continued to grow and develop but we still had our work cut out for us. Actually, since I worked overseas, *Kelly's* work was still cut out for her. Being away was hard, but I also came to really appreciate everything I had in my life and I couldn't be happier. As time went on, we stuck to our plan of keeping in touch while I was away. I just had to ride out the next few months and hope nothing catastrophic happened. Fingers crossed!

CHAPTER 16

Longest Rotation Ever

AS LONG AS I can remember, my rotations overseas have either gone really fast or really slow. I remember back in 2006 doing a thirteen-month rotation and not realizing I was in the country that long until my shift leader made me take leave—not that I felt burned out or anything. I felt fine and would have kept going until my next scheduled leave. That was during the cowboy days of running Baghdad. When you're on a solid team with guys you trust with your life, there is no other place in the world you want to be. Plus, at the time, I was single and really had nothing better to do.

I've also been on sixty-day rotations where it felt like I was there for a year and it never seemed to end. It had nothing to do with the team I was on, but I either had something urgent to do at home or the operation tempo catches up to you. What sometimes wears me down is the administrative load that usually came down the line. This was no more true than from 2009 to 2011 when a lot of changes went down in Blackwater's upper management and being a contractor became more of a "cooperative" relationship. I saw this as the start of the end of a good thing, and I made the switch from being a third-party contractor for the State Department to a direct hire.

At the State Department, I started in March of 2011 as a Security Protective Specialist. I immediately liked the way the program was being run and the doors it could open for me, but most importantly, from training until I left, I worked with some really solid guys and loved being overseas. I enjoyed it so much that even after I was blown up in Peshawar on September 3, 2012, and given the option to do anything I wanted after I healed, I not only went back to Peshawar to finish my tour but extended it an extra year. It was an easy decision.

What I failed to see at the time is that I missed out on the opportunity to go anywhere in the world. When I told the director of diplomatic security that I not only planned on going back to Peshawar but planned to stay longer, he was surprised but that decision pretty much solidified my reputation as a solid and honorable person. That reputation follows me to this day and helped set me up for a full-time career working with the State Department.

As noted earlier, my overseas rotations average ninety to a hundred days with a twenty- to thirty-day break in between. The rotation following Collin's birth would be longer—Feb. 6 to June 17—because I took eight weeks of Family Leave. I had to get back on a normal rotation, which meant seventeen weeks to play catch-up. At first it seemed to fly by, but at the four-week mark, I hit a brick wall.

When I first arrived back in Kabul on February 6, I jumped right into my routines and it seemed that time would fly by for me. I was working twelve-hour days, six days a week, and while that may seem like a lot, you have to remember that this is in Afghanistan. I can't just jump in a car and go out for ride or enjoy a meal at a local restaurant. My entire life pretty much took place at the embassy and there was always something to do between training for races back home and my studies in-between work shifts.

It's not that work was uninteresting. You never knew what would happen. First thing in the morning I would head to a secure room to get a briefing from the Assistant Chief of Mission (ACOM) on all the diplomatic motorcade movements and motor pool movements scheduled for the next forty-eight hours. I would often come up with reasons to cancel these activities for such things as reported threats or general security concerns. This was the best time to give the ACOM such recommendations based not just on the reports but also personal experience gained while working in Kabul for the last several years. Some people feel uncomfortable being in a position to make recommendations that in some circumstances may hinder US diplomacy, but in the end it's not only about the safety of the people we are protecting but also the safety of the security personnel going out on the actual movements. Many diplomats often forget about that, but that's what the State Department pays me for: to give honest, no-nonsense recommendations.

Once the morning ACOM brief is over, I head to the Embassy Protection Division (EPD) and we pretty much go over the same things except at a slightly lower level where I brief the shift leaders, let them know the concerns we had with certain movements, and get their view as well. It also gives us an opportunity to catch up on the prior day's movements and if there were any issues and, more importantly, address any issues that may come up in the next forty-eight hours. This meeting is more informal and if all goes well, only lasts about fifteen minutes.

The rest of my morning—at least until lunch—can be hit or miss but most days fly by because when you monitor twenty to thirty movements per day, there are a lot of moving parts as passenger, team, and vehicle formations change. I will also get a rundown from our "future operations" office to get their take on what the next forty-eight hours might look like and sometimes into the next seven to ten days, especially if we have VIPs coming to visit.

With all of this, I can still usually take care of some admin tasks and walk to lunch by 11:30. Throw in a kinetic event such as an explosion or high-profile attack, and all plans go out the window. At that point we let the situation develop and see how or if it impacts embassy operations. If the event has no impact, it becomes a chess game as I start to move things around to keep my people from getting stuck in traffic. If it does directly impact embassy operations, that's a much more complicated story but not one for this book.

As long as there are no surprises, I always walk to the farthest dining facility to get a little exercise, grab some food to go, then head back to the office and eat at my desk. So when I say my life is routine, I'm not kidding because with the exception of unforeseen "events," just about every minute is planned out. At the same time, the routine is what makes the rotation go quickly. However, once you hit that four-to-six-week mark, your tolerance for the stupid gets really short.

A good example of this is the toaster at the dining facility. For some reason, the working locals and guard force get the crazy idea to put tortillas in the toaster oven, and since toaster ovens are mainly designed for, I don't know, TOAST! they get stuck and burn, hence a lot of smoke and it ruins toast-making for everyone. Oh, and they get the same result when they try to warm up cookies. I'm getting fired up again just thinking about it.

Another irritation is food. We have four different dining facilities on the compound and they're free, meaning you can eat as much as you want with just the swipe of a card. (To say that the embassy has a high proportion of people with weight problems is an understatement.) On the embassy intranet site, they list the menus for the entire week for all the dining facilities to make it easier to figure out where you want to eat and also when to eat to avoid long lines. But they sometimes mix up the menus and don't serve what's advertised. When you look forward to, say, chicken parmesan and they are serving fish, it's disappointing at first, but after two or three months can really set you off.

After lunch, the day more or less goes by in a flash because you start prepping everything for the next forty-eight hours. And as regular operations begin to slow down in the late afternoon—following my 2 p.m. espresso break—I'm able to start wrapping things up and prepping for the next shift depending on how many people we have on ground. This has always been one of the reasons I enjoy working out prior to my shift because at the end of the day, I'm smoked and try to go to bed as early as possible.

I'm not sure if it's PTSD or just all my years of being overseas, but my sleep schedule is messed up. When I first get back from leave, I don't have any issues sleeping, which might be due to jet lag. But after about a week that shit goes right out the window, and I can't get more than three or four hours a night for a couple of days until my body gives out and I pass out for a good eight to ten hours. I wake up feeling refreshed, but then the cycle starts all over again.

Me and five other guys rotate between different shifts throughout a rotation so everyone gets a little break. There's the morning shift from 6 a.m. to 6 p.m., the mid/overlap shift from 10 a.m. to 10 p.m., the night shift from 6 p.m. to 6 a.m., and what we call Future Operations which usually runs from 7 a.m. or 6 p.m. Since none of these shifts are written in stone, we adjust as needed, and as long as there's a butt in the hot seat 24/7, our leadership leaves us alone.

I like to start my rotations on the mid-overlap shift for a week or so, then the morning shift for a month, another month in Future Operations, and wrap up my rotation on night shift so it's easier to adjust to the time difference once I get home. We all have our favorite shifts; I'm happy to work any of them but Futures and nights are my favorite.

Nights shift are the most interesting because after hours at a US Embassy can be very entertaining—you never know what may happen, especially on Thursday nights because Friday is an off day and as I've said more than once, Foreign Service Officers love to party. I've dealt with maintenance issues, noise complaints, robberies, medical emergencies, and even suicides, and death by assault. Some people get stuck in the elevator, which I always find amusing. Most of the people at the embassy don't seem to realize that since it's US Government property, you are always being watched, like a running image on social media. There is always evidence if you do something stupid.

The weirdest shit happens during Future Operations. Just when you think you've seen it all, BAM! welcome to the show. This is where we screen all the request for movements within the City of Kabul and plan incoming VIP missions. In order to safely conduct these movements, we have what is called the Mission Security Travel Policy (MSTP), which is a required read for all new arrivals. It goes into great detail on the do's and don'ts of traveling in Kabul so you would think it's pretty cut and dry, but there's a lot to consider, such as current threats and the general atmospherics of the city, which are constantly changing. In the end, one of the best things about working in futures is that the schedule is set and the hours fluctuate based on how many travel requests and incoming VIP visits get submitted on a certain day.

One way or the other, I adjust my routine to ensure that everyone gets equal amounts of stress and downtime during a normal three- to four-month rotation and that I'm able to talk with Kelly by Skype and keep up with Collin's growth. Kelly has her own routines mothering Collin, Brett, and the two dogs while continuing to run the household without me being there. Have I already said I think she's awesome?

CHAPTER 17

Happy Father's Day

···

AS FEBRUARY turned into March and then April, May, and finally June, it was time to start my turnover. The last couple weeks at work flew by, and since I was able to wrap up my rotation on night duty, I felt both ready to go home and surprisingly well rested. All I had left to do was lock up my sensitive items, change the password on my work computer account so it doesn't expire while I am away, and set my out-of-office reply to make sure anyone needing to contact me is routed to whoever is covering for me. That's pretty much it.

The day I head out, I usually get up early and have a final crushing workout before catching the embassy chopper for the five-minute flight to the airport. Since travel around Kabul is risky, we use our embassy aircraft to bypass potential trouble. Once I arrive, there's enough time for lunch and waiting for my ride to the commercial aircraft side of Hamid Karzi International Airport (HKIA) to whatever country you're connecting through. My favorite flight path is Kabul to Dubai, Dubai to Dulles, and then Dulles to Bradley International in Connecticut. With the exception of the thirteen-hour flight from Dubai to DC, the overall trip is not that bad, about twenty-seven hours from start to finish. In Dubai I eat a good dinner, take a hot shower, and walk around for a few hours so that I'm pretty exhausted by the time I board the flight.

Compared to how bad I was feeling back in February, I can say looking back that this was not my worst rotation. I can't say the same for Kelly's "rotation," though—you'd have to ask her. I was also coming home in time for Father's Day, my first, and I was excited as hell but also nervous. The trip back was pretty much a breeze, and before I knew it, I was getting off the plane at Bradley and headed to where Kelly normally meets me. But I had a stop to make first.

Even though I took a shower, shaved, and put on clean clothes in Dubai, I'd still been traveling for over twenty hours and needed to clean up, so I headed straight to the men's room to wash my face, brush my teeth, and put on a clean shirt. I never worried about clean shirts in the past, but Kelly wanted to be sure I wouldn't transfer any of the crud I might have picked up while flying halfway around the world. And since Kelly had spent the last seven months making sure Collin didn't get sick, I didn't want to be the one who messed that up.

As nervous as I was, I couldn't wait to hug and kiss Kelly and hold Collin. I was amazed at the many different emotions that were coursing through me; I was anxious, scared, happy, and ready to cry all at the same time. It was one of the best feelings I've ever felt because I was able to experience everything. I felt truly at peace. Having such emotions for the first time also made me realize that even as an adult, you are always learning and valuing your life and what's in it.

Once I walked through security, I immediately started looking for Kelly and Collin. Two seconds later, there they were. I gave Kelly a big kiss and she handed me Collin and strong emotions flew through me as I hugged and kissed my little dude. Kelly had dressed him in overall shorts with a button-down shirt and a bow tie. He was pimpin'! I held him the entire way to the car and sat in the back with him all the way home. He did fall asleep after about ten minutes, and I just stared in amazements at how much he had grown.

The drive to the house from the airport takes a little over an hour. Once we got back, Kelly grabbed Collin and I went ahead and opened the doors because Clarice is always excited to see me. She jumps up and down and runs around in circles, and the last thing we wanted was for her to accidentally knock me over holding Collin. She calms down after about ten minutes, which gives me time to escape and take a shower and change.

As long as Kelly and I have been together, we started a ritual that my first and last meal when I was home would be sushi, and until Collin was born, we kept the tradition going strong. Now we get it to go. Once I got out of the shower, Kelly placed the order and was off to pick it up. She figured on taking Collin, but since I wanted to stay home, I told her I would watch him and since it was time for a bottle, I figured, "What could possible go wrong?"

Kelly had warned me that Collin needed to get used to me again and there was a high possibility that once he realizes mama's not around, he would freak. I'm thinking, hell, I've spent over fourteen years in a war zone; I can handle my own son for forty minutes while my wife picks up dinner. As Kelly left, I gave Collin his bottle and as he started to nod off, I'm thinking, *Damn, Cap, you got this.* And then out of nowhere, Kaboom! He started to cry and things got real very fast.

At first, he just seemed a little fussy, so I figured he needed to be burped. I gently put him over my shoulder and patted his back just like I did when I was home a few months ago. After a few taps he let out what I called his Homer Simpson burp, and I figured all was well. I put him back in my arm, but as I slipped the bottle back into his mouth, that was it. He wanted no part of it and started to cry. At first it was a light sob so I gently rocked him and that seemed to make things worse. Soon enough it was a full-on wail and I began to panic. As his crying became even worse he started coughing, and no matter what I did, nothing helped. I tried rocking, walking, talking, going out-side, dancing, and finally singing. He just kept crying.

Now I'm thinking it's time to call Kelly because this can't be good for him, but trying to use my cell phone while Collin was exploding was not going to happen, so now I'm at a total loss. I laid him on the carpet on his blanket which is what Kelly sometimes does when he's rolling around and having tummy time, but that made the crying even worse. Fifteen minutes later I made a des-perate attempt to finally get through to Kelly. What I didn't know is that she shuts her ringer off so it doesn't wake Collin up and she forgot to turn it back on when she left, so my cry for help fell on deaf ears. At this point I went into medic mode and came to the conclusion that if he's crying, he's breathing, so just ride out the storm.

After what felt like hours but in actuality was only twenty minutes, Kelly pulled into the driveway, and as I took Collin to the door to greet her, no sooner did I take a single step outside that he stopped crying and was suddenly all smiles. As I told Kelly what happened, she chuckled as I handed Collin off to her. I went to the car and grabbed the sushi. I'm not even home two hours before causing Collin to have a meltdown. I had four weeks left!

We both knew there would be a transition period after I got back, but neither of us expected the meltdown. But the rest of the night was really fun, and I enjoyed spending time with Collin. It hit me again how much I missed him, and it was a blast watching him sit up and play with his toys. I even put together his Jumparoo. It's a baby seat on springs that allows a baby to jump, and Collin seemed to love it. (It's actually pretty cool; I wish they made them for adults!) He didn't fully grasp the concept of jumping or spinning around in the seat, but it played music and that's all he needed, and there was that big grin again. I always have a smile on my face, so it seemed Collin was already taking after me.

sThe first night home was a bit weird for everyone. While I'm gone, Kelly, Brett, and Collin fall into their own daily routines. Then all of a sudden I'm back and throw a wrench in the whole thing. In the past I was always running out the gate wanting to help Kelly as much as I could, but all too often, I was making things worse and adding more stress. So over the years, I've learned to take a more laid-back approach the first week I get back and wait for Kelly to ask for help rather than jump right in. There are a few things I can do right away, which is to help her change Collin, feed him, and get him dressed, especially when we want to go out. Otherwise, I focus on working around the house and yard to get the things done that Kelly or Brett aren't able to do, and if I'm needed, I'm there in a flash.

That first week is also a time for me to adjust to being back home and syncing back up with my family and friends. I still tend to get up early in the morning to work out and it's nice to have a few minutes of quiet as the sun comes up. These moments are few and far between, though, because Collin will often get up early for a bottle and I never know what day that will be. He can sleep in for five days straight and I'm back in rhythm, but then he's up at 4:30. You just never know! The plus side is that because I'm an early riser, I can take care of Collin so Kelly can sleep in. I take him downstairs, change him, and give him a bottle. Once he's done with that he likes to play, so we spend the next couple of hours with his toys and watching cartoons. I have really come to enjoy this time and get a little disappointed if he doesn't wake up by 5 or 5:30. I really hope that as he gets older, he looks forward to it as much as I know I will.

As long as Kelly and I have been married, she has never known a normal life because from the day we met, I have always worked overseas. And to this day she has never complained about my job or the amount of time I'm away. Every time I return, she makes my homecoming special. One time she left our Christmas tree up until I got back in March so I could open presents in front of it. She also had a late birthday party for me months after the actual day. This year was no exception except it was even better because I got to hold my son on my first-ever Father's Day, and though words can't express what I was feeling, I can say this: when I met Kelly, I won the lottery.

After a while we all get back a comfortable routine. I'm able to be more helpful, and I can tell Kelly feels the relief as I start taking day-to-day stuff off her plate. I will go grocery shopping, run errands, and, more importantly, do more things around the house that she normally does. I know our dogs love my being back; Kelly will feed them when she gets up, but since I like to feed them as well and get up earlier, some days they get an extra breakfast.

It has always been a challenge coming home from a rotation and getting to know Kelly and Brett again. Now throw in Collin after a longer-than-usual rotation and I slowly began to realize that just because I'm away from work, I'm not on vacation, not at all. In fact, I have a new full-time job: strengthening my relationship with my family. But as the summer progressed and we all adjusted to me being back home, everything started to gel again and run smoothly. It was still difficult at times, but every day brought us closer and closer together.

CHAPTER 18

Sun's Out, Buns Out

·····

COLLIN AND I continued to bond, and I even talked Kelly into letting me take him for a spin around the yard on his four-wheeler which he seemed to have enjoyed. I thought of how fortunate I've been to have lived a unique life, and I hope to share it all with Collin. The lessons my father taught helped prepare me for the real world, and I'm grateful that he raised me the way he did.

Now that Collin was older and the weather better, we were able to take him out more often. We kept it pretty simple to help break him in little by little We came to realize it was all about timing, taking him out between meals, and driving to a store a little further away so he can nap in the car which keeps him from getting tired and cranky. We also took him out to eat a couple of times. We started out simple and took him to Panera because the food is quick and if he does have a meltdown, we can pack up and get out in a matter of minutes. Our strategy seemed to be working, everywhere except for Michaels. His favorite place is Walmart, but then who doesn't like going to Walmart? We thought about taking him to the zoo or the aquarium, but at his age neither of us figured he would get much out of it, so we decided to postpone bigger trips for a few more months.

Since Collin was born, I've scored a lot of great stuff off eBay. That site rocks! Although Kelly's not a big fan of it, the best thing I've bought is the Tactical Baby Carrier. It fits on your back and you can face him toward or away from you. It's also easy to move around since he's under thirty pounds and a perfect fit for it. It does use Velcro, which means Daddy has to put some patches on it, so I went with my good ol' Blackwater "Stop Screaming, I'm Scared Too" because in the end, you have to represent the bear paw.

What I also like about the carrier is its tactical design with lots of straps and buckles, making it easier to tuck him in there nice and snug or keep it loose. Plus, from all my years overseas wearing body armor and load-bearing vests that weighed forty to fifty pounds, I can roll with his little twenty-pound baby bod all day long, which frees up Kelly, and we don't have to push a stroller around. I can also be a goofy dad, free to jump around or whatever because Collin is safely attached. I'm not sales-pitching this thing, but I really like it.

It has been a remarkable journey from when we first brought Collin home until now, watching how a child grows and develops. What adults tend to take for granted must seem amazing to a baby: a certain sound, the taste of a new food, a new light or color. Each one is a brand-new experience for them. There's a good and bad to this, though, because they can just as easily become fixated on something horrifying as something that gives them pleasure. Fortunately for Collin, his experiences so far seemed pretty positive.

I noticed this on two occasions. The first was when Kelly got him a swing, and the second was the first time we put him in a swimming pool. We put him in a blue plastic swing with a chest and lap strap, let him sit in it for a bit, then slowly began to rock him. He got this big grin on his face, and in five minutes I was swinging him like Tarzan. The higher he went, the bigger the smile and louder the laugh. It became the perfect summer thing because we could sit outside and swing him after his bottle and have a family dinner at the same time. We also used the swing for nap time; five minutes after we fed him, he was out like a light. We had to be careful, though, because if he wanted to go in the swing but wasn't occupied with something else, he would fall right to sleep which led to late nights and early mornings—still proving that no matter what, Collin set the schedule. Still, that thirty-dollar swing was worth every penny.

Now comes the pool. I'm not a big fan of the pool and would like nothing more than to fill it and call it a day. I used to love the water, but all my years in the Navy being cold, wet, and miserable made swimming something I dread. I still don't hesitate to jump in when I have to no matter how cold the water is, and I'll swim when I run my races, but give me a choice and I'll stay on the side. When Kelly and I went to the Bahamas on our honeymoon, we didn't go to the beach once. We did plenty of scuba diving but no swimming or beach time. But now throw in a child, and I learned pretty quickly that if they want to go in the pool, you're going in the pool.

Neither my mom or dad knew how to swim, and I only learned when I got involved in scouting. I taught both of my brothers and then Brett how to swim. I therefore assume that Collin will become one hell of a swimmer. But it's all about the baby steps and first making sure he's comfortable in the water. The last thing I need is for him to get scared and never want to go in the water again, which would mean it would be harder to enjoy it as he got older.

So we keep him in the shallow end and glide him around and he mostly seems to like it. With the solar cover on most of the day and the pool in a location that never gets shade, the water temperature breaks 85 by the end of June and by the end of July gets up in the 90s, so there's little chance of Collin getting cold. And since he's still in diapers and not mobile enough for pool diapers, we just strip him down and put him in naked. Turns out the kid loves to skinny dip, so right off the bat he's just like his dad. When Kelly and I take him in the pool, we call it "sun's out, buns out" time. Who doesn't love swimming naked?

We have found that the best time to take Collin to the pool is after six in the evening because the sun is starting to go down and the water is still nice and warm but not the hottest. It's also a chance for some quality family time. I have come to appreciate the simple things in life, and it's amazing how swimming in the pool with my family for an hour or so after dinner is one of the biggest parts of being home that I enjoy. It's worth all the sacrifices I've made by working overseas. To see the joy on everyone's face and knowing that I'm providing this for my family is the greatest gift in the world.

By next summer when Collin's a little older, I'll start teaching him how to swim. Even though I've come to hate water, I swim like a fish and can tread water for hours without even thinking about it—which is my goal for Collin so he'll never have to worry about being in the water whether it's a river, a lake, or the ocean. I want to make sure he's not only a good swimmer but able to read a situation and know if the water is safe or not.

I'm usually home about every other summer; sometimes I can catch the May to June time frame and others the August to September, but June to July is hit or miss. That's one of the biggest reasons this summer is so special for me since it's Collins very first summer and what started out a little rough is going well, and I really feel like our father-son bond is starting to develop. It made me wonder what it will be like when I have to leave again, but this time it would be different because out of the blue, I was given the chance to go back to Iraq. After spending the last five years in Kabul, I was ready for the change.

Is there really a difference between Iraq and Afghanistan? The short answer is a big fat YES! But only because I'd be working at the US Consulate in Erbil; I wouldn't go back to Baghdad for anything. Erbil is located in Northern Iraq—also known as Kurdistan – and it's a huge difference. As soon as you cross that imaginary line it's a whole new world. The Kurds are great; what I like the most is their generosity, especially toward Westerners. Whether the locals identify religiously as Sunni, Shia, Muslim, Christians, or Jew, they consider themselves Kurds above all else, and that's what matters. There are shopping malls, restaurants, fast food joints, and theaters, they sell alcohol, and the local women can dress any way they want, whether in traditional covering or Western style clothing. Western investors have helped to create a booming economy, and it blows your mind. It's hard to believe you are even in Iraq.

I would go back to Kabul for a few weeks to check out and ship my things to Erbil, then home for a couple of months for training and to wait for my Visa and country clearance. If all went well, I would leave for Kabul by July 16 and still get another month or so of vacation before heading to Erbil in early November.

I was excited for the new opportunity and honored to have been selected. In Kabul, my staff and I were responsible for protecting up to seven thousand US citizens and I worked ten to twelve hours a day, seven days a week. In Erbil I would work a more normal schedule and only be responsible for a couple hundred people. As great as all of that was, I was most stoked about coming right back home in just six or seven weeks.

As much as I work out, I also consider our family to be active and look forward to making sure Collin continues the tradition. We're often outside doing stuff and take him on daily walks up to three miles depending on where we go. One of our destinations is the town's Hampton Hill Cemetery. There are a lot of old cemeteries in New England and more so where we live due to the history of the area. From what I understand, our town was founded around 1715 but didn't incorporate until 1786 Some of the original homes tell that story and ours is one of them. There are no records, since none were kept until 1789, but you can tell by the construction that the main part of our house was built in the mid-1700s.

Kelly has been into old cemeteries for as long as I've known her, so when she wanted to become a mortician, I wasn't surprised. Whatever town we're in, she likes to walk around the old cemeteries and it's a great time to get Collin outside. Sometimes when we walk to the Hampton Hill Cemetery, we start at the top of the hill and go down to the cemetery's main gates and wander around inside. It's about a mile walk of pushing his stroller, sometimes on wet grass, and I always have my Tactical Baby Carrier just in case. It's like a timeline to see all the old headstones and dates and what people said on them (when you can read them). I don't think there is anyone famous from Hampton, but the history is still pretty cool.

As I go about the daily routines balancing chores with Collin time, I'm amazed at how much I enjoy doing things with him. It can be as simple as going to the attic to grab some gear for a race or putting him in the carrier to take out the trash. I just have fun being with him. Every day he seems to do something new or experiences something for the very first time, and the look of pure amazement and joy warms my heart. The shit-eating grin he gets when you take him in the pool with his butt hanging out is one of the funniest things of all, but I think he just likes to pee in the pool.

CHAPTER 19

They Sure Grow on You

···

AS I'VE SAID, the more time I spend with Collin, the more we bond, but I can't touch the connection he has with Kelly. Fortunately, from what everyone tells me, father-son bonding really starts as the kid gets older and becomes more active and independent. And anyway, Kelly will be the one person he sees every day; dad will be the person he sees a few times a year. It kind of sucks, and I keep reminding myself about the bigger picture and what's best for my family. I hope that, as he gets older, he will understand.

Still, the longer I'm home, I can tell how much more comfortable he becomes with me, to the point where I can take him while Kelly is doing something around the house or runs to the grocery store or for gas. When he starts getting cranky, we go outside, I put him in his swing, and I gently push him, which usually mellows him out. It generally takes about thirty to forty minutes before meltdown if he realizes that Kelly's not around, but she's usually back by then. When Kelly is close by and he gets eyes on her, I can take him outside and he's good to go. If he starts to worry, Kelly will hold him for a few minutes and then pass him back to me. We still haven't reached the point where Kelly can leave for a *long* period of time, but hopefully as he gets older that will change.

One of the hardest things for me is finding time to be with Kelly. Collin gets up early and often in the middle of the night, but if he goes to bed by seven or eight, then Kelly and I can take showers and relax. But since we are always on the go, if we stop for more than twenty to thirty minutes, we end up falling asleep. Balancing time between Collin and Kelly is my biggest challenge, and I sometimes feel I'm failing as both a husband and father. I'm not yet sure what to do about that, but at the end of the day I always ask myself, "Did I try to do the right thing?" And I usually look in the mirror and tell myself, "Maybe, but I can do better." I'm getting there. Just put one foot in front of the other and learn from my mistakes.

One of the things I look forward to as Collin gets older is taking him with me when I go places, like to the gym or store or out with friends or just for a hike. Growing up, my father took me everywhere and always supported me in the things I wanted to do, and I will do the same for Collin. When I wanted to go scuba diving, my dad supported me. Same for both skydiving and rock climbing. He would call my bluff when I wanted to try something but gave me the opportunity to do it. Even though I got toys and clothes for Christmas and birthdays, by the time I was seven or eight, I started showing interest in bigger adventures. Soon I was getting camping equipment and one year I got a tomahawk. Later I had my own .22 rifle and 20-gauge shotgun. This way I was able to go to the range with my dad and to shoot trap and skeet. By the time I was sixteen, I was not only an Eagle Scout but a certified scuba diver, novice rock climber, and had one tandem skydive under my belt.

I look at the type of person I've become, and it had a lot to do with how I was raised by my parents. I also now know that each kid is unique and what worked for me may not work for Collin. I will certainly expose him to as many new things as possible, and whenever he shows an interest in something—especially the kinds of activities I enjoyed growing up—I will look forward to spending that quality time with him. But I won't push my son into doing anything he doesn't want to do. My father, for example, was an avid hunter, but as he realized I showed no interest in it, we went fishing and to the range more often. I found I enjoyed trapping, which was something he didn't know much about but was interested in learning, and it became another activity we were able to do together. Now I don't plan on turning Collin into a trapper, but since we do live on thirty acres of land, there will be plenty of adventures for us to explore.

It's not only hard to balance my time between Collin and Kelly, but I also want to stay connected to Brett. Brett was raised a lot differently than I was, and it has been challenging for us to bond, especially as he's getting older. We just don't share the same interests. He also has a "real" dad he spends time with, and it doesn't help that I work a million miles away. I do try to be a good role model for him such as being a good husband and teaching him how to be a responsible person. We also have our weekly breakfast which is going strong to this day and we finally found a great place near home that serves pancakes the size of a small pizza. And while he doesn't enjoy running races like I do, he goes with me without complaint and has been a big help, from the World's Toughest Mudder to my Spartan Races. We always have a good time when we go out to dinner and he really seems to enjoy these road trip adventures. It's been nice to have him along and he's turning into one hell of a young man.

The bond I see Brett and Collin forming is great. You could tell he wasn't thrilled when we first told him that Kelly was pregnant. He had this crazy idea that he would be changing diapers and staying up all night because Collin would cry every hour, but I kept telling him that Collin would impact us all, and he wouldn't have to do any of those things. Not to mention Brett sleeps like a rock and can't even hear his alarm go off for school.

I'm looking forward to when Collin gets a little older so he can join Brett and me when we do stuff. I plan on keeping our Tuesday breakfast ritual, and Brett even asked when I thought Collin would be old enough to join us. I'm thinking maybe eighteen to twenty-four months, but only time will tell. If Brett wants his brother to come to breakfast with us, then I'm all for it. It would also give me a chance to get Collin into "breakfast mode," because I know that as Brett grows up and moves on, going to breakfast will slowly fade from a weekly thing to maybe a monthly or yearly. Heck, maybe it will be something I get to do with Brett and *his* children. That would be cool.

Something else I know is that as Collin gets older and our bond strengthens, there will come a time—and I dread the day—when he asks me why I'm gone from home so much. That conversation will break my heart. But there's a light side to all of this. Having a child in my late forties has been challenging, but it has completely changed my perspective and motivation about being overseas. I've been fighting the "War on Terror" for more than seventeen years and never thought I'd give it up. I love my job, and I believe in making sacrifices for my country and family. I believe in the values of our country and would give my life for freedom without a moment's thought.

Collin's birth did not change those views because I know my sacrifice is for the greater good of us all. There have been a few close calls, but God has not seen fit to cash in my chips yet. But now that Collin's in my life, I want to enjoy time with him and watch him grow up and hopefully share some of my values with him. I did my time and I'm ready to pass the watch over to someone else. I still have five years left and a lot could happen during that time, but to finally have a goal and endpoint in sight puts me at peace. Both Kelly and I are still very happy with my decision.

So when I finally hang up the gun belt, I will have more than thirty years of combined military and federal service behind me. I'll know that I did my part and am lucky enough to have survived with a hope to live in peace for the remainder of my years. Well, maybe not "peace"; one of the first things I plan to do is buy a tractor and turn my property into a true farm. Now I have no clue how to farm or what I'm going to grow, but I'll be retired with plenty of time to figure it out. This also means I'll get to stay home with Collin and take care of things for Kelly the same way she took care of us over the years. Not only that, since Kelly and I have a ten-year age difference, she's agreed that I can spend extra time with Collin while she works. Even though we are blessed to be in a situation where she can stay home full time if she wants, she loves to work and it kills her that she hasn't been able to.

This kind of arrangement is apparently becoming more normal. The problem, at least for some of my retired friends, is that after a couple of years they start to go a bit nuts because they can't find enough to do. I worry about that for me because I know boredom will slowly creep in, especially as Collin gets older. I often laugh at my worst-case scenario that I'll become a "CrossFit Mom" like some of the ladies in my 9 a.m. class who've just dropped their kids off at school. Fortunately, I have plenty of experience and even now am offered consulting work for a month here and there both in the US and overseas. I'm also looking at converting my education into a teaching certificate, and I discovered while writing this book that I enjoyed the process and would like to keep writing. So maybe my retirement won't be so boring.

Collin getting older does scare me because I was forty-five when he was born. I think that's one of the reasons I go out of my way to eat right and stay in shape: so that I'll be able to keep up with him and be there as he experiences the world. This is very important to me. Since I enjoy taking Brett to my races, I'm hoping that as Collin gets older, the three of us can go. This way, as Brett gets too old to hang out with me, Collin will be right there. Brett was twelve when I started dragging him to my races, and from what Kelly has said, he enjoys it. So let's do the math—when Collin is twelve, I'll be fifty-seven. Will I still be running obstacle course races? Only professional athletes or people who have spent their careers in the military know how hard it is on your body. I hurt in places that I did not even know could hurt: my knees, elbows, shoulders, and every other joint in my body. It takes about forty minutes and a hot shower each morning to get everything unstuck and moving before I start my day.

I know I've made multiple comments on the pages about how Kelly feels about my active lifestyle and how crazy she thinks it is, but that's just how I am. Once I focus on something, I go for it. I wish I was more like this when I was younger since my competitive nature didn't fully develop until my early thirties. What would I have been like as such a kid? I was motivated back then, don't get me wrong. But my focus was on Scouting, getting good grades, and developing skills I would need in the military because I never wanted to be an athlete; I just wanted to jump out of planes and blow shit up. Working out was just something you had to do to stay mentally and physically strong.

When it comes to athletic ability, I'm not sure what Collin will possess. Will he have Kelly's coordination from her skills at ballet or my drive and determination? I know I can't catch, throw, or dribble any type of ball to save my life, but when it comes to running, climbing ropes, and overcoming obstacles, I'm part monkey and part bull. I just don't have any quit in me and would rather give 100% to come in dead last than not participate at all because of my weaknesses. That drive is how I tackle everything; it has helped make me the person I've become. If Collin gets any of that, he should be good to go.

I do feel that since both Kelly and I are short, so too will Collin be, and I hope that never discourages him when it comes to trying new things. I never let my height bother me, and to tell you the truth, I never really thought of it until I was old enough to start dating and then realized that being taller would have improved my success rate. But I did meet Kelly.

The more time I spend with Collin, the more I realize that the simple things are all that matter to me: having breakfast, watching cartoons, playing with toys, giving him his bottle, noticing those moments when he laughs or smiles. I don't think it will ever replace what he has with Kelly, but as he gets older and I'm able to share more experiences with him, our bond will keep getting stronger. I know I enjoyed every moment I spent with my father and can only hope and pray that Collin will feel the same way toward me.

CHAPTER 20

Until Next Time

....

AS I WRAP UP my trip back home and head back to Kabul for my final rotation, a new chapter of my life is opening up, and I often wonder where it will take me. The world is one strange place and you never know what could happen. Being a father has turned my life completely upside down in ways I would never have imagined. It's an experience one can never understand until you actually have children of your own, and it's different for moms than dads, especially if you're a first-timer.

I had just assumed that since Kelly already had Brett, it would be the same with Collin, but that is clearly not the case. Not only is every child different, but so is where you are in life when the child is born. Her circumstances are a lot different now than when she first had Brett, and she's able to spend more time with him. And I can already tell that her bond with Collin is even stronger than it is with Brett. Now that's not a bad thing, it's just the result of different circumstances. As a first-time mom, Kelly still had to work and go to school so her mother became the primary caregiver, which made Brett's relationship with his grandmother that much closer. Fast-forward to today, and because I have a good job and am away for work much of the time, Kelly has the freedom to stay at home and raise both Collin and Brett.

Throughout the last year, from learning that Kelly was pregnant to the emergency C-section and the months that followed, I've been constantly on the go and it has started to wear me down. In the past I had the luxury of enjoying my downtime when being home, but that world is gone. I start working almost as soon as I land in Kabul, and it's pretty much the same when I return home. If I want time to myself to do the things I've always enjoyed, I have to give up sleep. Once I'm home, between training, my races, the honey-do list around the house, and spending time with Collin, suffice it to say that I catch up on my rest back in Kabul since I have a reliable routine there. With Collin around, there are no reliable routines other than his feedings. I'm sure that will change as he gets older, but for now I will stick to getting up at 4 a.m. to start my day and going to bed when he does by 8 p.m.

I'm still hoping that the three of us will be able to share adventures. I remember that even with the seven- and fourteen-year age differences between my brothers and me, we would still do stuff together with our dad. I enjoyed spending time with my brothers and teaching them things I learned from our father. I still remember taking my youngest brother Sal rock climbing when he was about six; neither my father nor stepmother had any issues with me dangling Sal off a cliff a few hundred feet above the ground. After I joined the military, I had even more to teach them such as different shooting techniques.

I do have to keep reminding myself that I was raised in the late 70s and early 80s and what made sense then may not be acceptable today. With Collin I will just have to figure it out. Either way, he's in for the time of his life, and as long as he displays maturity and sound judgment as he gets older, he'll get that much more freedom to explore. I try to do the same for Brett, but he's already pretty independent and a lot different than when I was a kid. Still, he keeps testing the water for what he can and can't get away with, and as a young boy myself, I can relate to why he does certain things.

In general, I tend to take the same approach my father took with me: being completely honest. If you're acting stupid, you get called out. My father never once told me I was stupid, but there were plenty of times he would tell me I was acting like it. It's the only approach I know, and I tend to stick with it when it comes to Brett, and the success rate has been about 50/50. Kelly doesn't really like it when I confront Brett like that, but there have been a couple of times when he's told me later that even though he hated my honesty, he appreciated how it helped him get the point. In the end, I put him in a position where he knows exactly what he needs to do and it's totally up to him. I let him be in control of the outcomes, whether it's staying up late or wanting to go on a trip or driving our old truck around the field.

The challenge for me is making sure I stick to my promise when he meets the goals we set for him. It gets a lot harder when it comes to longer-term goals since I may be away at work and have to rely on Kelly to keep me posted. Of course, Brett will tell me he's being good and everything is moving forward while Kelly will give me an opposite report. I end up having to play detective to determine what actually happened. It's not because I don't trust Kelly; it's just that people can have a different point of view in the way they see things.

So the next big question is whether this approach will work with Collin, and I guess I'll find out. I'm already seeing the character of both Kelly and me in him, especially when it comes to his temper. He certainly has my happy-go-lucky demeanor, but in a split second he'll throw a fit and, according to my mom, that is exactly what I did. This temperament has served me well in the military because I've been able to stay calm under pressure and then instantly flip into heat mode to fit a situation. I have been on missions when one second I'm joking and relaxing with my team during prep and then as soon as we hit the wire, BAM! it's Donkey Kong time.

Despite all the time I've spent overseas fighting the GWOT (Global War on Terrorism) and countless debriefings by clinical psychologists, everyone is amazed that I haven't experienced any type of PTSD or damage from long-term exposure to combat. I think it's because I'm able to shut things off when I need too. I also like to stick to a routine, which gives me some stability; if it gets broken for any reason, I tend to get anxious. PTSD is tricky, though, and while I don't show obvious signs of it, I do notice a numbness to certain feelings.

So I'm not perfectly healthy. I may suffer some kind of low-level PTSD, there's the Traumatic Brain Injury, and in a few years, I'll be pushing fifty. But as long as my physicals are solid, that's good enough for me. I just need to convince Kelly that I'm A-Okay. When it comes to raising Collin, I not only want to be a good father and teach him how the real world works but to also help him find that balance where you can enjoy life, work hard, and take shit seriously when you have too. Finding that proper balance is easier said than done.

While growing up, my family had property in upstate New York, and with the exception of Christmas, we would spend every holiday there. I remember those times as if they happened yesterday. Thanks to my father, it's where I learned how to hunt, fish, camp, and be an outdoorsman. Both of my brothers had little four-wheelers by the time they were five and we would take family rides around the mountain. My brother Chris would ride with Dad and after Sal was born, Chris got his own bike and Sal rode with dad. Even now those memories bring a smile to my face. As I've said, our father might not have been keen on traditional parenting, but he sure prepared me for the real world.

As I wrote above, I know that Collin will have his own interests, but I hope he will end up with some of these same memories—hanging out in the woods with dad, learning about life in ways that most kids don't get to experience. It should be easier with all the property we own, and in a way I've already started, strapping Collin into his Tactical Baby Carrier and taking him for rides on our four-wheeler.

As I tackle this thing called parenting, I have to admit there is no easy way to do it, and what works for others most likely won't work for you. If parenting was easy, every kid in the world would grow up to be perfect and that's just not how it works. Sure, there are terrible parents out there and people in this world who shouldn't have children. But most of us are doing our best. As long my child is safe and has clothes on his back and food in his belly, I can check the box of being a decent parent. But that may be the easy part.

The hard part is that being a good provider isn't enough when it comes to raising kids. A good parent is also a good mentor who sets good examples and that's not always easy. I have to remind myself that I'm not with my buddies on a mission and I can't "mother——" everyone I see who pisses me off. I have to show restraint when dealing with jerks. My father was very direct; I saw him grab people by the throat if he felt they deserved it. When I was younger, I worshipped my father. But as I got older, I realized he wasn't able to read certain situations and got into trouble when he could have avoided it.

It may be okay to throat-punch a bad guy, but you have to pay attention to your surroundings and realize that there are better and worse ways to react to a situation, especially when your kid is around. Be clear about what you want him or her to learn and know the difference between right and wrong. Not every kid should turn out like their parents. I'm obviously no expert in any of this, but I do know that in the end, we each have to make our own decisions and live with the consequences.

Another part of parenting I plan to pass on to Collin is to respect not only his beliefs but those of others. I was brought up to treat everyone the way I wanted to be treated no matter their race, gender, religion, or sexual orientation. That is something I strongly believe in to this day even with the crazy times we are going through. And while it's always important to respect the views of others, you also need to believe in and respect your own, because there will always be those who see things differently, which doesn't make one person right and another person wrong. I really hope Collin learns to appreciate this.

As time goes on, I pray that I become a good parent and role model not only to Collin but to Brett. I know I still have a lot to learn, but hopefully with a little luck, they will both grow up to be responsible adults who have learned to survive in this world. Then I know I will have done my job. But who knows what the future holds for any of us?

Until next time…